EXECUTIVE EDITOR
Natalie Earnheart

CREATIVE TEAM
Jenny Doan, Natalie Earnheart, Christine Ricks,
Tyler MacBeth, Mike Brunner, Lauren Dorton,
Jennifer Dowling, Dustin Weant, Jessica Toye,
Kimberly Forman, Denise Lane, Gunnar Forstrom

EDITORS & COPYWRITERS
Nichole Spravzoff, Camille Maddox,
Annie Gailbraith, David Litherland,
Julie Barber-Arutyunyan, Hillary Doan Sperry

SEWIST TEAM
Jenny Doan, Natalie Earnheart, Courtenay Hughes,
Carol Henderson, Janice Richardson,
Aislinn Earnheart

PRINTING COORDINATOR
Rob Stoebener

PRINTING SERVICES
Walsworth Print Group
803 South Missouri
Marceline, MO 64658

LOCATIONS
Lee and Kelly Durbin, Hamilton, MO
Evelyn Dowling, Hamilton, MO
Caldwell County Historical Society, Kingston, MO
Caldwell County Courthouse, Kingston, MO

CONTACT US
Missouri Star Quilt Company
114 N Davis
Hamilton, MO 64644
888-571-1122
info@missouriquiltco.com

Oops! Sometimes we make mistakes. To find corrections to every issue of BLOCK go to: **www.msqc.co/corrections**

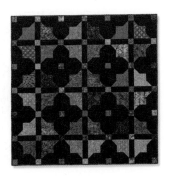

A note from Jenny

"In diversity there is beauty and there is strength."
— *Maya Angelou*

Dear Quilters,

Strolling through a fabric shop is still one of my very favorite things to do. The vibrant bolts of fabric stacked on the shelves are all so beautiful. I always find new prints I can't live without (and I'm sure you do too!). It would be so dull to walk into a fabric shop and see only one type of fabric in one monotonous color. Thank goodness there are so many styles, colors, and prints to enjoy! I feel the same way about all of you and the wonderful quilts you create. If I only saw one type of quilt in the same color palette for the rest of my life, it would be a disappointing sight. I love diversity and all the beauty you bring to this world by just being who you are.

This issue of Block features beautiful quilts from a group of extraordinary quilters that I deeply admire. I am continually astonished by all the unique ways you do what you love. Quilting is so adaptable—you can use found scraps of fabric or big, color-coordinated bundles of fat quarters and still create marvelous works of art. Whether you prefer to play by the rules and stick with patterns or you adore freestyle piecing with improvisational quilt blocks, you are expressing your individuality in a meaningful way.

Thank you for sharing your stories and your lovely creations with us. By celebrating our distinct gifts and contributions, we find, as Maya Angelou said, "In diversity there is beauty and there is strength." I gain strength from all of you as you fearlessly spread joy through your creativity.

Jenny

JENNY DOAN
MISSOURI STAR QUILT CO.

Modern Masters of Quilting: The Gee's Bend Quilters

Almost 20 years ago, the tiny, rural community of Gee's Bend was brought into prominence when their quilts were discovered to be works of art, not just the simple bed coverings they'd always believed they had been making. Their quilts were purchased by collectors and displayed in art museums across the country causing quilting to be elevated from folk art to masterpieces. In one of the first reviews of their artwork in 2002, Michael Kimmelman of the *The New York Times* called the Gee's Bend quilts "some of the most miraculous works of modern art America has produced" comparing them to renowned artists like Henri Matisse and Paul Klee.

The exceptional modern art style of Gee's Bend quilts might be attributed in part to their unique community. Their isolated town is nestled in a crook of the Alabama River, surrounded on three sides by water without a bridge or ferry. Being a close-knit group of only a few hundred, the quilters of Gee's Bend have passed on their knowledge and skill to subsequent generations, untouched by outside influences, allowing their patterns and variations on patterns to live on. In their insular community, they have taken traditional quilt blocks and molded them to fit their own preferences with astonishing results.

Another reason the Gee's Bend quilters' style is so unique is their utilitarian spirit. They are a make-do group of women who have taken old work clothing, worn out blue jeans, scraps of corduroy left over from a sewing contract with Sears in the 70s, and just about any kind of fabric they could get their hands on, to make their incredible abstract quilt designs. Without the means to simply buy fabric, they made their scarcity into a feast for the eyes.

They design innately, inspired by their surroundings and what they have on hand, creating organic quilt compositions that go far beyond the precise, mail-order quilts they had once produced back in the 1960s for the Freedom Quilting Bee to sell in department stores like Bloomingdales and Saks 5th Avenue. They allow their quilts to wibble and wobble. The colors alternate as they see fit. They don't have straight borders. These quilts don't play by the "rules."

It's such a pleasure to marvel at the improvisational prowess of the Gee's Bend quilters—a surprising addition of yellow blocks in a mostly blue, brown, and maroon quilt is a welcome sight. A half-log cabin quilt with blocks turned this way and that feels so freeing. Rows and rows of blue jeans with faded knees turns into a master work when discarded work pants are pieced together just as

Photography by Arthur Rothstein, 1937. Photo courtesy of Souls Grown Deep.

they are, allowing them to speak clearly of their origins. In the Gee's Bend quilts are innumerable variations of the well-known "housetop" quilt block, that many of us might recognize as "courthouse steps," a variation of the log cabin. They take this block that is built strip by strip, and add vibrant centers or ignore the centers altogether, focusing more on the contrast of light and dark in the strips themselves. They add a few pieces of striped fabric for interest wherever they please. Patterns and solids are used in wildly varying combinations and the

Housetop & Bricklayer Blocks With Bars Quilt by Lucy T. Pettway, 1955. Photography by Stephen Pitkin. Photo courtesy of Souls Grown Deep.

*Bars & String-Pieced Columns Quilt by Jesse T. Pettway, 1950s
Photography by Stephen Pitkin. Photo courtesy of Souls
Grown Deep.*

*Lucy T. Pettway. Photography by David Raccuglia.
Photo courtesy of Souls Grown Deep.*

colors just seem to work. After taking in such freely interpreted designs, we hope you feel yourself filled with the desire to play with fabric again, cut it without squinting at the markings on a ruler, and sew it together without a pin in sight. Why not? There are no mistakes to be made when you simply allow yourself to create.

Souls Grown Deep

Ever since their quilts have been discovered to be the works of art they truly are, the quilters of Gee's Bend have experienced a renaissance of creativity in their community. Those who had long since put down the needle and thread have picked it up again in the fervor of renewed quiltmaking, and those who had never been interested in the art of making quilts before suddenly found themselves longing to be a part of this vibrant group of quilters. All were welcomed in and during the past 20 or so years, more quilts have been made than ever before. And they're just as beautiful and inspiring as we remember.

To help this community continue to promote their art and to protect the livelihoods of these quilters, Souls Grown Deep has partnered with Nest to help the quilters of Gee's Bend. The Nest team has spent time in Gee's Bend with the quilters there, building relationships and getting to know these wonderful

women to help them market their world-renowned quilts and make sure their unique stories are heard.

More than half of the population in Gee's Bend struggles with poverty. Many don't have internet access in their homes and as a result, it has hindered their ability to connect with those outside their community and reach a wider audience to sell and to display their quilts. Souls Grown Deep, with their partner Nest, is working with these wonderful quilters to help them receive fair payment for their quilts and build a strong foundation for future financial success.

We took a moment to chat with Rebecca van Bergen, the Founder and Executive Director of Nest, a nonprofit organization that's committed to preserving the rich cultural history and value of crafts, while creating a more inclusive makerspace through greater opportunities for artisans across the globe who otherwise may not be well-represented.

What led the Gee's Bend quilters to be represented by Nest?

"Nest understands and celebrates the historical and cultural significance of the quilts being stitched in Gee's Bend, and is eager to elevate the voices of the quilters, their stories, and the heritage of this important craft community. As America seeks a brighter future for all of

Photography by Edith Morgan, 1900. Photo courtesy of Souls Grown Deep.

its people, we are committed to ensuring that art and craft are represented in the evolution of our social identity.

To that end, we are seeking philanthropic partners that can lend their resources, platforms, and expertise to marginalized artisans to ensure that all makers' voices can be heard, and that no craft heritage is left behind."

What is important for us to know about the work these renowned quilters do?

"The women of Gee's Bend—a small, remote, Black community in Alabama—have created hundreds of quilt masterpieces dating from the early 20th century to the present. The some seven hundred or so inhabitants of this small, rural community are mostly descendants of slaves, and for generations they worked the fields belonging to the local

Pettway plantation. Quiltmakers there have produced countless patchwork masterpieces beginning as far back as the mid-nineteenth century, with the oldest existing examples dating from the 1920s. Enlivened by a visual imagination that extends the expressive boundaries of the quilt genre, these astounding creations constitute a crucial chapter in the history of American art."

What has changed for the Gee's Bend Quilters since their quilts have become well-known in the quilting community and in the world?

"While these quilts have earned the Gee's Bend community national, even global, recognition, the fame of this important heritage craft has not translated into economic advancement for residents of The Bend. Historically, their only

Jessie T. Pettway. Photography by David Raccuglia. Photo courtesy of Souls Grown Deep.

"The women of Gee's Bend … have created hundreds of quilt masterpieces dating from the early twentieth century to the present."

Lazy Gal Variation Quilt by Arcola Pettway, 1976. Photography by Stephen Pitkin. Photo courtesy of Souls Grown Deep.

"They design innately, inspired by their surroundings and what they have on hand ... these quilts don't play by the rules."

Bars & Strips Quilt by Mary Lee Bendolph, 2002. Photography by Stephen Pitkin. Photo courtesy of Souls Grown Deep.Photo courtesy of Souls Grown Deep.

opportunity to sell their quilts was when visitors made their way to this isolated town or when their quilts were selected for representation in a gallery, which has hindered business growth and ongoing sustainable income for the many quilters who are still actively practicing their craft. The opportunity to share their work digitally presents a new future for the quilters of Gee's Bend: the chance to realize the economic potential they deserve and allow consumers all over the world the chance to see—and own—these masterpieces."

How can we help support the work of the Gee's Bend quilters?

"During the COVID-19 pandemic it's been increasingly difficult to access Gee's Bend, and support the work of the community. However, we have worked to establish online shops for interested quilters to expand their reach and promote their stories and goods. Nest will also conduct a series of in-person training and educational services for program participants. These efforts will empower the quilters to share their artwork with a wider digital community who are not encumbered by the ability to get to the Bend."

In light of recent events, what kind of support does the Gee's Bend community need?

"Establishing an eCommerce presence is essential to the long-term economic success of the quilters, their families, and their community. Beyond that, being able to promote and market their crafts to an audience that appreciates their beauty, craftsmanship, and heritage is critical to protecting the cultural value of these goods. This website will allow both the historic legacy and the incredible art still being created to be celebrated as archival images, oral histories, and visual storytelling assets. Together, Nest and the quilters of Gee's Bend, will launch a marketing campaign to ensure visibility and increased exposure for the makers and quilts and help earn the shop attention, notoriety, and following."

To learn more about the Gee's Bend quilters check out their Instagram at @geesbendquilters. To view their quilts online and purchase their works of art please visit:

www.buildanest.org/geesbend

www.etsy.com/featured/black-history-month#gees-bend

Gee's Bend Inspired Bonus Pattern

Housetop Hoopla Quilt

We designed this fun bonus quilt, inspired by the quilts of Gee's Bend. Each block was made by our own employees of Missouri Star Quilt Co. resulting in this beautiful quilt. We hope this inspires you to create your own!

materials

BLOCK SIZES
- 9½" unfinished, 9" finished
- 18½" x 9½" unfinished, 18" x 9" finished

SUPPLIES
Varies

SAMPLE QUILT
Uses various fabric scraps

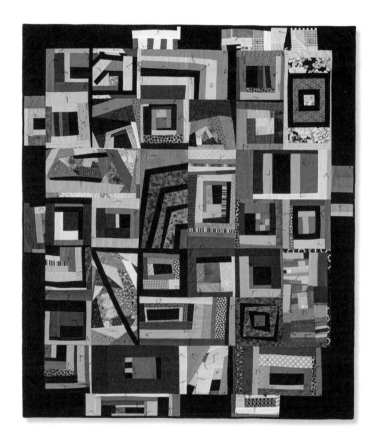

1 setting up parameters

Assigning rules or guidelines will lead to a successful project. Our sample quilt was created by a group of 12 makers, but these parameters could be helpful even if you are making a quilt like this by yourself.

We requested our makers follow a few basic parameters:

- *Parameter #1:* Create an improv log cabin block.
- *Parameter #2:* Use a little bit of black fabric somewhere in each block.
- *Parameter #3:* Blocks need to be 1 of 2 sizes—square blocks need to finish at 9" and rectangular blocks need to finish at 18" x 9".

2 basic block construction

Sew your first log side to 1 edge of your central piece. Press the seam towards the log side and trim if necessary. **2A**

Sew the next log side to the adjacent edge of the unit. Press towards the new log side and trim if necessary. **2B**

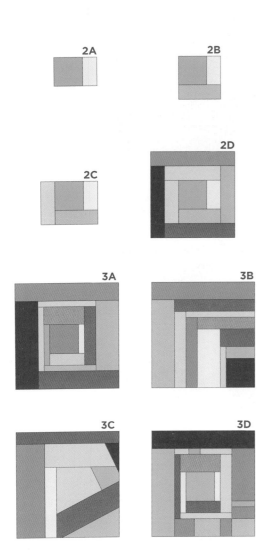

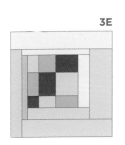

Continue adding log sides, pressing, and trimming until your block measures your desired size. **2C 2D**

3 block variations

You can use more than 1 variation in each block if you like. Experiment with those that you like and ignore the ones you don't!

Variation #1: Using different sizes of logs results in a very dynamic block. **3A**

Variation #2: You can alter the number of log sides and vary the number of logs on each round you sew! **3B**

Variation #3: Create a wonky-looking block by sewing on logs at any angle you like. **3C**

Variation #4: Some of the blocks in our quilt have logs that were made from smaller pieces sewn together. **3D**

Variation #5: You can use any shape with 4 sides or even piece fabric together to create a pieced center. **3E**

4 arrange & sew

Determine the arrangement that works best for the blocks you are using in your quilt. Sew the blocks together to create the rows. **Note:** If you have 2 sizes of blocks like our quilt, you'll need to sew the smaller ones together to create larger blocks and form the rows.

Press the seams of the rows in opposite directions. Nest the seams and sew the rows together.

5 border

From the border fabric, cut the number of strips needed to frame your quilt. These strips should be ½" wider than the desired width of your finished border. We had an odd number of blocks to create our quilt. We pieced the center of the quilt and then used the remaining blocks in the border. To do this, trim the remaining blocks to measure the same width as the border strips you just cut.

Sew the border strips and the trimmed blocks together to form 1 long border strip. Cut the border pieces from this strip. Refer to Borders (pg. 118) in the Construction Basics to measure, cut, and attach the outer borders.

6 quilt & bind

Layer the quilt with batting and backing then quilt. After the quilting is complete, square up the quilt and trim away all excess batting and backing. Add binding to complete the quilt. See Construction Basics (pg. 118) for binding instructions.

A Quilted Farewell
Disappearing Four-Patch Weave Quilt

This past year has brought a lot of changes to our lives; some good, some, well, less than ideal. Though, if this year has shown us anything, it's that we need to send love and care to everyone we know! And we quilters know how to send love through our sewing and quilting projects. This story by Janice Gritz that she shared on our Facebook page tells us about how love (and quilting!) keeps you going when you're off to a new chapter in life:

"In early 2017, as we were packing up our house to move to NW Washington from Tennessee, my cousin texted me that she had something to give me that needed to be delivered in person. She said, 'Your kids will appreciate this, because they know our family history and mine don't know my California family history.' So I warned her of all the moving mess and she drove up from Texas with the bundle, which turned out to be a lovely quilt with embroidered signatures. It was beautiful and I recognized and had met most of the people although I was a child at the time. Linda told me she'd found the quilt among her mother's things after her mother had passed. We figured she'd gotten it from her mother, our grandmother, who had passed away when I was just two years old.

"The quilt is pristine; whites don't stay white on a quilt for 100 years unless it is cherished and put away carefully. I figure the quilt was given to my grandmother on the occasion of the family leaving Missouri sometime in 1920 for the oil fields of California. My grandfather and my dad's oldest brother left Missouri in 1918 to go out and see if there was work, and they found it north of Los Angeles in a little farming community about 20 miles from the Pacific Ocean. They worked in the oil fields and saved enough so that Grandma and the three kids left at home (my dad was the youngest) could come out on the train. My dad was 11 years old at the time, so they didn't have to buy him a ticket; he was supposed to sit on his mom or sister's lap the whole way. That story always made us laugh as kids, trying to imagine my dad sitting on my Aunt Ressie's lap.

"Looking at the signatures on the quilt, I see my grandma's sisters and brothers and in-laws, and a close friend from church. Grandma, so far from home and her whole family, must have loved it very much. I can see her taking it out and tracing over the signatures and remembering the faces and good times. I take it out now and then and remember them, too. It's good to know where you come from."

materials

QUILT SIZE
75" x 82½"

BLOCK SIZE
8" unfinished, 7½" finished

QUILT TOP
1 package 10" print squares
1 package 10" background squares

INNER BORDER
¾ yard

OUTER BORDER
1½ yards

BINDING
¾ yard

BACKING
5 yards – vertical seam(s)
    or 2½ yards of 108" wide

SAMPLE QUILT
Flea Market by Lori Holt for Riley Blake

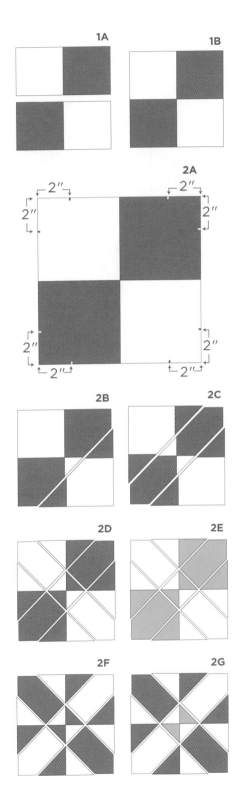

1 make 4-patches

Set 6 print squares and 6 background squares from your packages aside for another project.

Cut each of the remaining print and background squares in half vertically and horizontally, creating (4) 5" squares from each square. Keep the prints in pairs of 2 matching 5" squares for a **total of 72** pairs.

Arrange a pair of matching print squares and 2 background squares in a 4-patch as shown. Sew the units together in 2 rows. **1A**

Press towards the print squares. Nest the seams and sew the rows together to complete the 4-patch. Press to 1 side. Square to 9½" if needed. **Make (72)** 4-patches. **1B**

2 block construction

Hint: A rotating cutting mat or small cutting mat that can be turned is helpful for making multiple cuts without disturbing the fabric.

Lay a 4-patch unit on your cutting surface. Measure and mark 2" from each corner along both edges. **2A**

Lay your ruler atop the 4-patch and cut the diagonal line connecting the marks just made on the right edge of the unit, 2" from the top, to the bottom edge of the unit, 2" from the left. **2B**

Without disturbing the unit, cut the remaining diagonal line connecting the marks from the top right to bottom left. **2C**

Without disturbing the unit, cut twice on the opposite diagonal, similar to how you made the diagonal cuts before. **2D**

Carefully move the cut unit to the side for the moment. In the same manner, measure, mark, and cut a second 4-patch—twice on both diagonals. **2E**

Keep the pieces cut from the same unit together and switch the placement of the print and background corner pieces as shown. **2F**

Trade the center units from the first cut 4-patch with the second. **2G**

Lay a print corner facing up. Lay the right triangle section on top lining up the bottom and right edges. Notice that the background edge of the triangle is next to the print corner edge. Sew along the right side. **2H**

Press open towards the print corner. The outer edges will not line up evenly. **2I**

In the same manner, add the left triangle to the left side of the print corner. **Make 2** triangle sections. **2J**

17

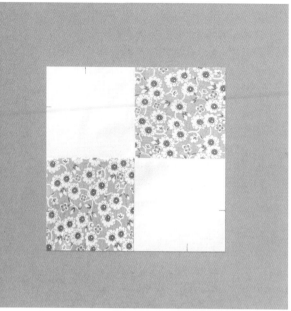

1 Lay a 4-patch unit on your cutting surface. Measure and mark 2″ from each corner along both edges.

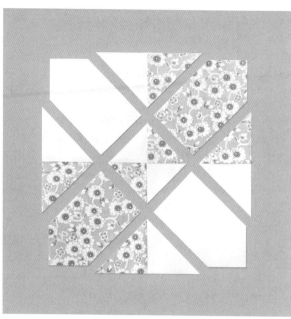

2 Cut the diagonal line connecting the marks on the right edge of the unit, 2″ from the top, to the bottom edge of the unit, 2″ from the left. Cut the remaining diagonal line connecting the marks from the top right to bottom left. Cut twice on the opposite diagonal. Repeat to mark and cut another 4-patch unit.

3 Switch the placement of the print and background corner pieces as shown. Trade the center units from the first cut 4-patch with the second.

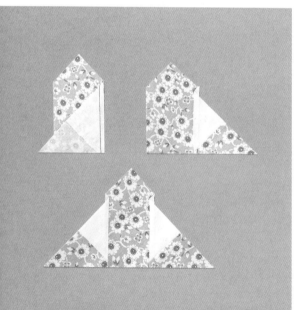

4 Lay the right triangle section on top of a print corner, lining up the bottom and right edges. Sew along the right side. Press. In the same manner, add the left triangle to the left side of the print corner. Make 2 triangle sections.

5 Sew the background corners to either side of the center unit as shown. Note that the center unit is turned so that the prints are next to the background corners. Press towards the background corners.

6 Arrange the 2 triangle sections and center section as shown. Nest the seams and sew the sections together. Press.

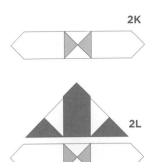

2K

2L

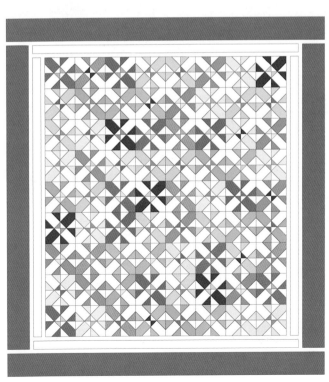

2M

Sew the background corners to either side of the center unit as shown. Note that the center unit is turned so that the prints are next to the background corners. Press towards the background corners. **2K**

Arrange the 2 triangle sections and center section as shown. Nest the seams and sew the sections together. Press. **2L 2M**

Measure 4″ from either side of the vertical and horizontal center seams and trim the block to 8″ square. **Make 72** blocks. **2N**

Block Size: 8″ unfinished, 7½″ finished

3 arrange & sew

Refer to the diagram below as necessary to lay out your units in **9 rows** of **8 blocks**. Notice that the blocks alternate turning 90° creating print and background *X*'s. Sew the blocks together in rows.

Press the seam allowances of all odd-numbered rows to the left and all even-numbered rows to the right. Nest the seams and sew the rows together. Press to complete the center of the quilt.

4 inner border

Cut (7) 2½″ strips across the width of the inner border fabric. Sew the strips together end-to-end to make 1 long strip. Trim the inner borders from this strip.

Refer to Borders (pg. 118) in the Construction Basics to measure, cut, and attach the inner borders. The strips are approximately 68″ for the sides and approximately 64½″ for the top and bottom.

5 outer border

Cut (8) 6″ strips across the width of the inner border fabric. Sew the strips together end-to-end to make 1 long strip. Trim the outer borders from this strip.

Refer to Borders (pg. 118) in the Construction Basics to measure, cut, and attach the outer borders. The strips are approximately 72″ for the sides and approximately 75½″ for the top and bottom.

6 quilt & bind

Layer the quilt with batting and backing then quilt. After the quilting is complete, square up the quilt and trim away all excess batting and backing. Add binding to complete the quilt. See Construction Basics (pg. 118) for binding instructions.

A Hug from Great-Grandma
Double Square Star Four-Patch Quilt

Quilts leave a legacy that can last far beyond the lifespan of their creators. As we pass down quilts, we connect generations. For Brenda Bristow, that connection stretched all the way back to her great-grandmother!

"Almost seventy years ago, my great-grandmother started work on a quilt that was to be a gift for my mother's upcoming wedding. It was a Double Wedding Ring made with scraps, including many original 30s prints, and a poly-cotton background fabric. She stitched all the arches, cut most of the melons and ring centers, and assembled two rows of six rings. Then she suffered a stroke.

"Her daughter—my grandmother—dutifully packed all the pieces in a box. She gave the box to my mother, telling her she would have to finish the quilt herself. Neither my mother nor my grandmother quilted, so the box sat in Mom's cedar chest for over thirty years.

"Fast-forward to the 1980s. After passing a quilt shop on my way to and from work every day, I finally signed up for quilting classes. Three years later, I got married, left my job, and moved to a new city with my husband. Mom suggested I tackle the Double Wedding Ring to fill some of my newly-found free time, but those curved seams scared me, so the box sat in my stash untouched.

"Eighteen years and many quilting classes later, my eldest daughter got braces. I needed a hand sewing project to keep myself busy during her many appointments, so I decided to pull out the Double Wedding Ring and piece more rings. I managed to add a few more rows to Grandma Matthews' work, and fully intended to finish the quilt, but I allowed other projects and activities to stall it once more.

"Finally, in 2015, I started meeting with a small group of ladies from my Smocking Guild chapter to sew at a quilt shop every Friday. This time, I was determined to finish the quilt! My friends offered encouragement and advice, even suggesting needles that worked the poly-cotton more easily. Shortly thereafter, my mom had a health scare. She knew I had been working on the quilt and challenged me. 'I'd really like to see Grandma Matthews' quilt finished before I die.'

"Finally, for her birthday in 2018, I presented my mother with her last wedding gift from her grandmother—and me. More than six decades had passed since the quilt was started. The top was completely hand pieced, and I learned how to free-motion quilt on my home machine to finish it off. I felt I had my great-grandmother's guidance and permission to complete her work.

"The quilt now covers the guest bed in my mother's house, so I and her other guests, including my younger daughter, have slept under the quilt.

"When I gave my kids quilts for their first college apartments, I told them sleeping under the quilt was like a big bedtime hug from me. This special Double Wedding Ring quilt is a hug from Grandma Matthews too."

materials

QUILT SIZE
63" x 75"

BLOCK SIZE
12½" unfinished, 12" finished

QUILT TOP
2 packages 5" print squares
¾ yard accent fabric
1¾ yards background fabric

INNER BORDER
½ yard

OUTER BORDER
1¼ yards

BINDING
¾ yard

BACKING
4¾ yards – vertical seam(s)
   or 2½ yards of 108" wide

SAMPLE QUILT
Blue Stitch by Christopher Thompson for Riley Blake

1 cut

From the accent fabric, cut (10) 2½" strips across the width of the fabric. Subcut each strip into (16) 2½" squares for a **total of 160** accent squares.

From the background fabric, cut (24) 2½" strips across the width of the fabric.
- Subcut 14 strips into 2½" x 6½" rectangles. Each strip will yield up to 6 rectangles and a **total of (80)** 2½" x 6½" background rectangles are needed.

- Subcut 10 strips into 2½" x 4½" rectangles. Each strip will yield 8 rectangles and a **total of (80)** 2½" x 4½" background rectangles are needed.

2 snowball rectangles

Fold each 2½" accent square on the diagonal and press a crease. **2A**

Lay a marked 2½" accent square atop a 2½" x 4½" rectangle as shown, right sides facing. Sew along the marked diagonal line and trim the excess fabric ¼" away from the seam to snowball the rectangle. Press towards the snowballed corner. Repeat to snowball a **total of (80)** 2½" x 4½" rectangles. We'll call these short rectangles for clarity. **2B 2C 2D**

Lay a marked 2½" accent square atop a 2½" x 6½" rectangle as shown, right sides facing. Notice the diagonal is the opposite direction from the 2½" x 4½" rectangles. Sew along the marked diagonal line and trim the excess ¼" away from the seam to snowball the rectangle.

Press towards the snowballed corner. Repeat to snowball a **total of (80)** 2½" x 6½" rectangles. We'll call these long rectangles for clarity. **2E 2F 2G**

Set the snowballed rectangles aside for the moment.

2A

2B

2C

2D

2F

2E

2G

23

1 Lay a marked 2½" accent square atop a 2½" x 4½" rectangle as shown, right sides facing. Sew along the marked diagonal line and trim the excess fabric ¼" away from the seam to snowball the rectangle. Press. Repeat to snowball a total of (80) 2½" x 4½" rectangles.

2 Lay a marked 2½" accent square atop a 2½" x 6½" rectangle as shown, right sides facing. Sew along the marked diagonal line and trim the excess ¼" away from the seam to snowball the rectangle. Press. Repeat to snowball a total of (80) 2½" x 6½" rectangles.

3 Layer a 5" print square atop a differing 5" print square right sides together. Sew down 2 sides. Cut the sewn squares in half vertically. Open to reveal 2 strip units. Repeat with the remaining 5" print squares. Press toward the darker fabric.

4 Select 2 differing strip units and layer 1 unit on top of the other with the seams lying horizontally. Sew down the 2 sides perpendicular to the seams. Cut the sewn squares in half vertically. Open to reveal (2) 4-patch units. Press. Make (80) 4-patch units.

5 Sew a short rectangle to the left side of a 4-patch as shown. Press towards the rectangle. Sew a long rectangle to the top of the 4-patch/rectangle unit as shown. Press towards the long rectangle to create a quadrant. Make 80 quadrants.

6 Arrange 4 quadrants in a 4-patch formation as shown. Sew the quadrants together in rows. Press the seams in opposite directions. Nest the seams and sew the rows together. Press to complete the block.

3 make 4-patches

Set (4) 5″ print squares aside for another project.

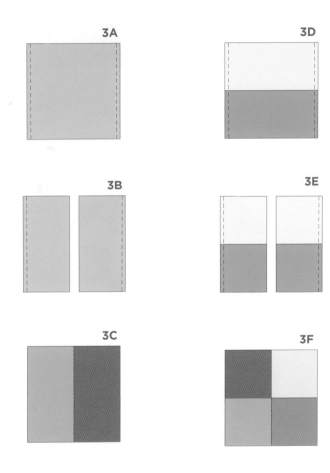

3A

3B

3C

3D

3E

3F

Layer a 5″ print square atop a differing 5″ print square right sides together. Sew down 2 sides of the stacked squares. **3A**

Measure 2½″ from either side and cut the sewn squares in half vertically. **3B**

Open to reveal 2 strip units. Repeat with the remaining 5″ print squares. Press the seam allowances of each strip unit toward the darker fabric. **3C**

Select 2 differing strip units. With seams running horizontally and right sides together, layer 1 unit on top of the other. Sew down the 2 sides of the strip units, perpendicular to the seams. **3D**

Measure 2½″ from either side and cut the sewn squares in half vertically. **3E**

Open to reveal (2) 4-patch units. Press the seam to 1 side. **Make (80)** 4-patch units. **3F**

4 block construction

Sew a short rectangle to the left side of a 4-patch as shown. Press towards the rectangle. **4A**

Sew a long rectangle to the top of the 4-patch/rectangle unit as shown. Press towards the long rectangle to create a quadrant. **Make 80** quadrants. **4B**

Arrange 4 quadrants in a 4-patch formation as shown. Notice the orientation of the quadrants within the 4-patch. Sew the quadrants together in rows.

Press the seam of the top row to the left and the seam of the bottom row to the right. Nest the seams and sew the rows together. Press to complete the block. **Make 20**. **4C 4D**

Block Size: 12½" unfinished, 12" finished

5 arrange & sew

Refer to the diagram on page 27 as necessary to lay out your units in **5 rows** of **4 blocks**. Sew the blocks together in rows.

Press the seam allowances of all odd-numbered rows to the left and all even-numbered rows to the right. Nest the seams and sew the rows together. Press to complete the center of the quilt.

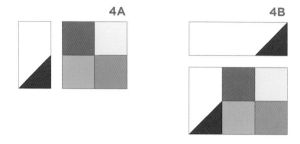

4A 4B

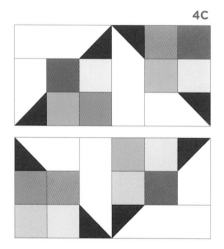

4C

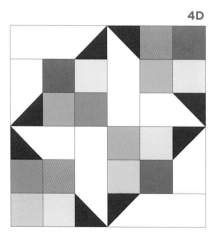

4D

6 inner border

Cut (6) 2½" strips across the width of the inner border fabric. Sew the strips together end-to-end to make 1 long strip. Trim the inner borders from this strip.

Refer to Borders (pg. 118) in the Construction Basics to measure, cut, and attach the inner borders. The strips are approximately 60½" for the sides and approximately 52½" for the top and bottom.

7 outer border

Cut (7) 6" strips across the width of the outer border fabric. Sew the strips together end-to-end to make 1 long strip. Trim the outer borders from this strip.

Refer to Borders (pg. 118) in the Construction Basics to measure, cut, and attach the outer borders. The strips are approximately 64½" for the sides and approximately 63½" for the top and bottom.

8 quilt & bind

Layer the quilt with batting and backing and quilt. After the quilting is complete, square up the quilt and trim away all excess batting and backing. Add binding to complete the quilt. See Construction Basics (pg. 118) for binding instructions.

A Fresh Start
Hourglass Wreath Quilt

It's finally a new year! As we leave 2020 behind, many people want to "get back to normal" and continue on the way things were in "the before times." I figure it's better that we learn from what we go through, and start fresh with a new perspective! So here's some tips for starting this new year off on the right foot:

Make Manageable New Year's Resolutions

Everyone's tried to make big changes when the calendar flips over, and big changes are hard! Instead of resolving to cut all that weight we gained or quilt a gigantic project in record time, let's give ourselves some grace and take baby steps to a better year. Make a more manageable resolution that turns into a daily practice like, "I'm going to get outside and walk around the block after lunch today," "I'm going to clean out one of my fabric bins," or "I'm going to work on my quilt for 15 minutes today." It's these little bits of progress that add up, and before you know it, you'll be better off than you ever were!

Reach Out to a Friend

We've all been a bit cut off from each other for a while now. One silver lining to this past year, though, is that it's easier to reach out to friends and loved ones than ever before. Check up on what those cousins are doing, or give a call to an old friend. Join a virtual quilting class and post photos of your progress. Participate in your local guild online. Plus, you could even send your friends a little handmade gift or a thoughtful note to connect with them again! We all need a chance to get social again.

Take Time to Do the Things You Love

Many of us have had an excess of free time this last year, and as things start to go back to business as usual, we're all going to suddenly be busier with our errands than we would like to be. Make sure to set some time aside for your hobbies and projects, whether they're long time favorites or something new you picked up last year. You'll be surprised at what you can do with just fifteen minutes a day. Sit down to sew just one block and before you know it, you'll have an entire quilt finished!

Of course, we can never know what a new year will bring. The only thing we can do is hope for the best and plan for the rest! What tips do you have for the New Year? Let us know on our Facebook page, or email us at blockstories@missouriquiltco.com to share your plans for the next year.

materials

QUILT SIZE
77" x 93"

BLOCK SIZE
14½" unfinished, 14" finished

QUILT TOP
1 package of 10" print squares
 - includes cornerstones
1 package of 10" background squares

SASHING
1½ yards background fabric

BORDER
1½ yards

BINDING
¾ yard

BACKING
5¾ yards – vertical seam(s)
 or 3 yards of 108" wide

SAMPLE QUILT
Solstice by Sally Kelly for Windham Fabrics

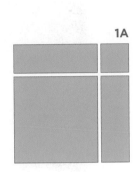

1A

1B

2A

2B

1 sort & cut

From your package of 10" print squares, select 20 squares for the block centers. Choose an additional 20 print squares and set them aside for the hourglass units. Set the 2 remaining print squares aside for another project.

Hint: A rotating mat or small cutting mat that can be turned without disturbing the fabric will come in handy for cutting.

From each of the squares chosen for the block centers, cut a 2½" strip from 1 side. Without disturbing the fabric, cut a 2½" strip across the top of both pieces creating (2) 2½" x 7½" rectangles, (1) 2½" square, and (1) 7½" square. **1A**

Subcut each 2½" x 7½" print rectangle into (3) 2½" squares. Keep matching prints together in sets of (1) 7½" square and (4) 2½" squares. **Make 20** sets and set them aside for the snowballed corners. Set the remaining 2½" squares aside for the cornerstones. **1B**

From each of (20) 10" background squares, cut (2) 4" strips across the width of the square. Subcut each strip into (2) 4" background squares. Each 10" square will yield (4) 4" squares and a **total of 80** are needed.

Set (20) 10" background squares aside for the hourglass units. Set the remaining 2 squares aside for another project.

2 snowball corners

Choose 1 set of (1) 7½" print square and 4 matching 2½" print squares and (4) 4" background squares. Set the 7½" print square aside for the moment. Mark a line from corner to corner once on the diagonal on the reverse side of each 2½" print square. **2A**

Place a marked square on 1 corner of a background square with right sides facing. Sew on the marked line. Trim the excess fabric ¼" away from the sewn seam. Press open towards the snowballed print corner. Repeat with the remaining marked squares and background squares to make a set of 4 matching snowballed units. Repeat to make a **total of 20** sets. Keep each set of snowballed units with the matching 7½" print square. **2B**

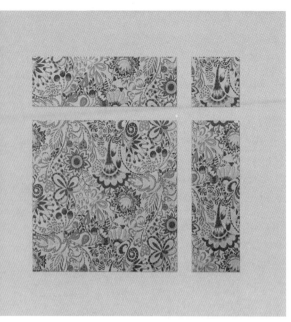

1 From each of the block center squares, cut a 2½" strip from 1 side. Cut a 2½" strip across the top of both pieces creating (2) 2½" x 7½" rectangles, (1) 2½" square and (1) 7½" square.

2 Subcut each 2½" x 7½" print rectangle into (3) 2½" squares. Make 20 sets of matching prints together in sets of (1) 7½" square and (4) 2½" squares. Set the remaining 2½" squares aside for the cornerstones.

3 Mark a line from corner to corner on the diagonal on the reverse side of each 2½" print square in your set. Place a marked square on 1 corner of a background square, right sides facing. Sew on the line. Trim the excess fabric ¼" away from the seam. Press.

4 Layer a marked background square with a 10" print square, right sides facing. Sew on either side of both diagonal lines. Cut the sewn squares in half vertically, horizontally, and along both marked diagonal lines. Open to reveal 8 half-square triangles. Press. Do not trim.

5 Place the marked half-square triangle atop an unmarked half-square triangle, right sides facing, print sides touching background sides. Sew on either side of the drawn line. Cut the sewn units in half on the drawn line. Open and press to reveal 2 hourglass units.

6 Sew the hourglass units together in pairs. Press. Arrange the double hourglass units, 4 snowball units, and center square in 3 rows of 3. Sew the units together in rows. Press. Nest the seams and sew the rows together.

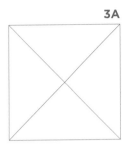

3A

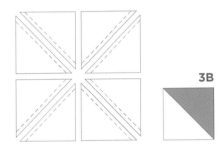

3B

3C

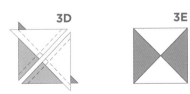

3D   3E

3 make hourglass units

Draw a line from corner to corner twice on the diagonal on the reverse side of the (20) 10″ background squares set aside for the hourglass units. **3A**

Layer a marked background square with a 10″ print square, right sides facing. Sew on either side of both diagonal lines using a ¼″ seam allowance. Cut the sewn squares in half vertically and horizontally and along both marked diagonal lines. Open to reveal 8 half-square triangles. Press each seam toward the print. Do not trim at this point. **3B**

Draw a line from corner to corner once on the diagonal on the reverse side of 4 half-square triangles. **3C**

Place the marked half-square triangle atop an unmarked half-square triangle, right sides facing. Nest the center seams and be sure to have print sides touching background sides. Sew ¼″ on either side of the drawn line. Cut the sewn units in half on the drawn line. **3D**

Each pair of half-square triangles yields 2 hourglass units. Repeat with the other half-square triangles to make a set of 8 matching hourglass units. **3E**

Note: When trimming, be careful to retain the corner points as you trim both sides of a corner.

If you are using the slotted trimmer, trim each unit to 4″, then open and press the seam allowance to 1 side. If you are not using the slotted trimmer, open each hourglass unit and press the seam allowances to 1 side. Measure each unit 2″ from the center point and trim to 4″ square.

Repeat to make a **total of 20** sets of 8 matching hourglass units.

4 block construction

Select 1 set of 8 hourglass units. Sew 2 hourglass units together, print sides touching, as shown. Repeat to **make 4** matching double hourglass units. **4A**

Select 1 set of (1) 7½" center square and 4 snowballed units that have prints differing from the double hourglass units. Arrange the units in 3 rows of 3, as shown. Sew the units together in 3 rows and press each row towards the double hourglass units. Nest the seams and sew the rows together. Press the seams in 1 direction to complete the block. **Make 20** blocks. **4B 4C**

Block Size: 14½" unfinished, 14" finished

5 make sashing strips

From the background fabric, cut (1) 2½" strip across the width of the fabric. Subcut (1) 2½" x 14½" rectangle and set the remaining piece of strip aside for another project.

From the remaining background fabric, cut (3) 14½" strips across the width of the fabric. Subcut (16) 14½" x 2½" rectangles from each strip. Add these to the previously cut background rectangle for a **total of 49**. Set 25 rectangles aside for vertical sashing rectangles.

Select 30 cornerstones from the stack of cornerstone squares set aside for sashing. Set the remaining 30 cornerstones aside for another project.

Arrange 5 different print cornerstones and 4 background rectangles as shown. Sew the pieces together in 1 long strip for horizontal sashing. Press the seams towards the sashing rectangles. **Make 6** horizontal sashing strips. **5A**

4A

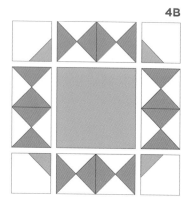

4B

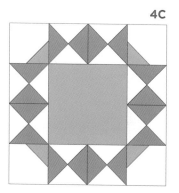

4C

5A

6 arrange & sew

Refer to the diagram on the left to lay out the blocks in **5 rows** with each row being made up of **4 blocks**. Place a vertical sashing rectangle in between the blocks and on both ends. Sew the blocks and vertical sashing rectangles together to form the 5 rows. Press the seams of each row towards the sashing rectangles. Place a horizontal sashing strip in between each row and on the top and bottom. Nest the seams and sew the rows and horizontal sashing strips together. Press the seams to 1 side to complete the quilt center.

7 border

Cut (8) 6" strips across the width of the border fabric. Sew the strips together end-to-end to make 1 long strip. Trim the borders from this strip.

Refer to Borders (pg. 118) in the Construction Basics to measure, cut, and attach the borders. The strips are approximately 82½" for the sides and approximately 77½" for the top and bottom.

8 quilt & bind

Layer the quilt with batting and backing then quilt. After the quilting is complete, square up the quilt and trim away all excess batting and backing. Add binding to complete the quilt. See Construction Basics (pg. 118) for binding instructions.

A Symbol of Freedom
Ohio Star Celebration Quilt

The story of the Ohio Star begins in a small Ohio college town by the name of Oberlin, just thirty-five miles southwest of Cleveland.

Oberlin has a rich history of social trailblazing. In 1835, the college became one one of the first in the country to admit Black students. Two years later, in 1837, it was the very first to admit women. By the mid 1800s, Oberlin was a center of the abolitionist movement and an important stop in the Underground Railroad. As such, Oberlin attracted many free-born and formerly enslaved Black families in search of education and opportunity.

In 1859, a man by the name of John Brown visited Oberlin to recruit antislavery soldiers. He hoped to spark a slave revolution by overtaking a Federal arsenal in Harpers Ferry.

Charles Langston, one of the town's most prominent Black citizens, felt the mission was destined to fail, but despite his warnings, two young Black men agreed to join John Brown.

One of those men was twenty-four-year-old Lewis Sheriden Leary. Lewis told his wife, Mary Patterson Leary, that he was traveling for business. He left her at home with their newborn baby and never returned.

Just as Charles Langston predicted, John Brown and his men were quickly defeated by the United States army. Lewis tried to escape by jumping into the river, but a hailstorm of bullets ended his life.

According to Mary's grandson, legendary poet Langston Hughes, "A friend brought [Lewis'] bloodstained, bullet-ridden shawl back to Oberlin. [Mary] still wore it fifty years after his death." Langston Hughes himself slept under the shawl as a boy. It was treasured as a symbol of Lewis' martyrdom.

An Ohio Star quilt was created in honor of Mary, Lewis, and all who sacrificed their lives in the fight for freedom. Mary's Ohio Star can still be seen at the International Quilt Museum in Lincoln, Nebraska.

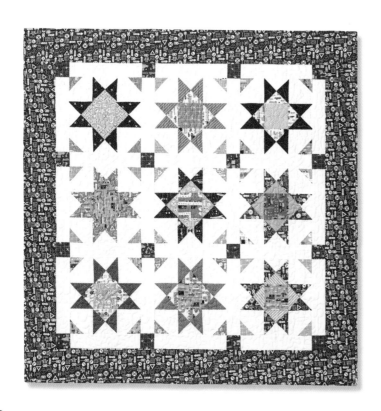

materials

QUILT SIZE
48½" x 48½"

BLOCK SIZE
11" unfinished, 10½" finished

QUILT TOP
2 packages 5" print squares
  - includes cornerstones
1¼ yards background fabric
  - includes sashing

BORDER
¾ yard

BINDING
½ yard

BACKING
3¼ yards - vertical seam(s)

OTHER
Clearly Perfect Slotted
  Trimmer B - optional

SAMPLE QUILT
On the Go by Stacy Iest Hsu
  for Moda Fabrics

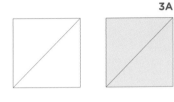

3A

3B

3C

3D

1 cut

From the background fabric, cut:

- (2) 5" strips across the width of the fabric.
  - From 1 strip, subcut (8) 5" squares.
  - From the other strip, subcut (1) 5" square. Set this with the previously cut squares for a total of (9) 5" background squares. Trim the remainder of the strip to 4" and subcut (6) 4" squares.

- (3) 4" strips across the width of the fabric. Subcut each strip into (10) 4" squares. Set these with the previously cut squares for a **total of (36)** 4" background squares.

- Set the remaining fabric aside for the sashing.

2 sort

Note: It is important to sort your squares before moving on to the next section to ensure you have the proper number of matching squares for each section. As you sort, stack the squares for each section and label each stack. We will reserve the remainder of the cutting for each section.

For the hourglass units, select 9 pairs of matching dark print squares, 9 light print squares, and the (9) 5" background squares.

For the snowballed corners, select 9 print squares and the (36) 4" background squares.

For block construction, select 9 print squares for the star centers.

For the sashing, select 4 dark print squares for cornerstones.

The remaining print squares can be used for a bonus project that you can find in the digital version of this issue.

3 make hourglass units

Pick up the stack labeled for the hourglass units. Draw a line from corner to corner once on the diagonal on the reverse side of each light print square and background square in the stack. **3A**

Select 1 pair of matching dark print squares, 1 light print square, and 1 background square from your stack. Layer a background square with a dark print square, right sides facing. Sew ¼" away from both sides of the drawn line. Cut the square in half on the drawn line. Open to reveal 2 dark print/background half-square triangles. Press the seams toward the darker print. **3B**

39

1 Layer a background square with a dark print square, right sides facing. Sew ¼" on both sides of the drawn line. Cut the square in half on the drawn line. Open to reveal 2 dark print/background half-square triangles. Press.

2 Repeat with a light print square and the matching dark print square to make 2 dark print/light print half-square triangles.

3 Place the marked background/dark print half-square triangle atop a dark print/light print half-square triangle, right sides facing, and dark prints touching either background or light print. Sew ¼" on either side of the drawn line, then cut on the drawn line. Open and press. Trim to 4" square.

4 Place a marked square on 1 corner of a background square with right sides facing. Sew on the marked line. Trim the excess fabric away ¼" from the sewn seam line. Press. Repeat to make a set of 4 matching snowballed units.

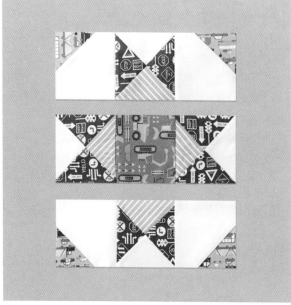

5 Select (1) 4" print square, 1 set of hourglass units, and 1 set of 4 snowballed units. Arrange the units in a 9-patch formation, as shown. Sew the units together in 3 rows and press each row towards the hourglass units.

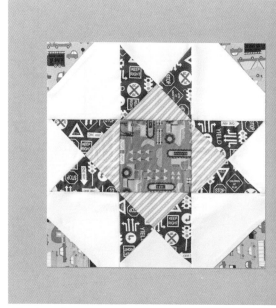

6 Nest the seams and sew the rows together to complete the block. Press 1 direction. Make 9 blocks.

3E

3F

4A

4B

4C

4D

Repeat with the light print square and the matching dark print square to make 2 dark print/light print half-square triangles. **3C**

Draw a line from corner to corner once on the diagonal on the reverse side of the dark print/background half-square triangles. **3D**

Place the marked half-square triangle atop a dark print/light print half-square triangle, right sides facing, and dark prints touching either background or light print. Sew ¼" away from either side of the drawn line. Cut the sewn units in half on the drawn line. **3E**

Each pair of dark print/background and dark print/light print half-square triangles yields 2 hourglass units. Repeat with the other half-square triangles to make a set of 4 matching hourglass units.

Note: When trimming, be careful to retain the corner points as you trim both sides of a corner.

If you are using the slotted trimmer, trim each unit to 4", then open and press the seam allowance 1 direction. If you are not using the slotted trimmer, open each hourglass unit and press the seam allowances to 1 side. Measure each unit 2" from the center point and trim to 4" square.

Repeat with the 8 selected print and background pairs to make a **total of 9** sets of 4 hourglass units. Keep the matching units together. **3F**

4 snowball corners

Pick up the stack labeled for the snowballed corners. Cut each print square in half vertically and horizontally to create 2½" print squares. Keep the sets of 4 matching 2½" print squares together.

Choose 1 set of 4 matching 2½" print squares and (4) 4" background squares. Mark a line from corner to corner once on the diagonal on the reverse side of each 2½" print square. **4A**

Place a marked square on 1 corner of a background square with right sides facing. Sew on the marked line. Trim the excess fabric away ¼" from the sewn seam line. **4B 4C**

Press open towards the print corner. Repeat with the remaining marked print squares and background squares to make a set of 4 matching snowballed units. **4D**

Repeat with the remaining 8 print squares and (32) 4" background squares to make a **total of 9** sets of 4 matching snowballed units.

5 block construction

Pick up the stack of print squares labeled for star centers and trim each to 4".

Select (1) 4" print square, 1 set of hourglass units, and 1 set of snowballed units. Arrange the units in a 9-patch formation, as shown. Sew the units together in 3 rows and press each row towards the hourglass units. Nest the seams and sew the rows together to complete the block. Press to 1 side. **Make 9** blocks. **5A 5B**

Block Size: 11" unfinished, 10½" finished

5A

6 make sashing strips

From the background fabric, cut (8) 2½" strips across the width of the fabric. Subcut each of the strips into (3) 2½" x 11" rectangles for a **total of 24**. Set 12 rectangles aside for vertical sashing rectangles.

Pick up the stack of cornerstone squares and cut each square in half vertically and horizontally to create (4) 2½" squares. You will need a **total of 16** squares for cornerstones.

Arrange 4 different print squares and 3 background rectangles as shown. Sew the pieces together in 1 long strip for horizontal sashing. Press the seams towards the sashing rectangles. **Make 4** horizontal sashing strips. **6A**

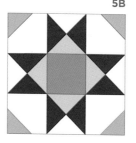

5B

6A

7 arrange & sew

Refer to the diagram on the left to lay out the blocks in **3 rows** with each row being made up of **3 blocks**. Place a vertical sashing rectangle in between the blocks and on both ends. Sew the blocks and vertical sashing rectangles together to form the 3 rows.

Press the seams of each row towards the sashing rectangles. Place a horizontal sashing strip in between each row and on the top and bottom. Sew the rows and horizontal sashing strips together. Press the seams to 1 side to complete the quilt center.

8 border

Cut (5) 5" strips across the width of the border fabric. Sew the strips together end-to-end to make 1 long strip. Trim the border from this strip.

Refer to Borders (pg. 118) in the Construction Basics to measure, cut, and attach the borders. The strips are approximately 40" for the sides and approximately 49" for the top and bottom.

9 quilt & bind

Layer the quilt with batting and backing then quilt. After the quilting is complete, square up the quilt and trim away all excess batting and backing. Add binding to complete the quilt. See Construction Basics (pg. 118) for binding instructions.

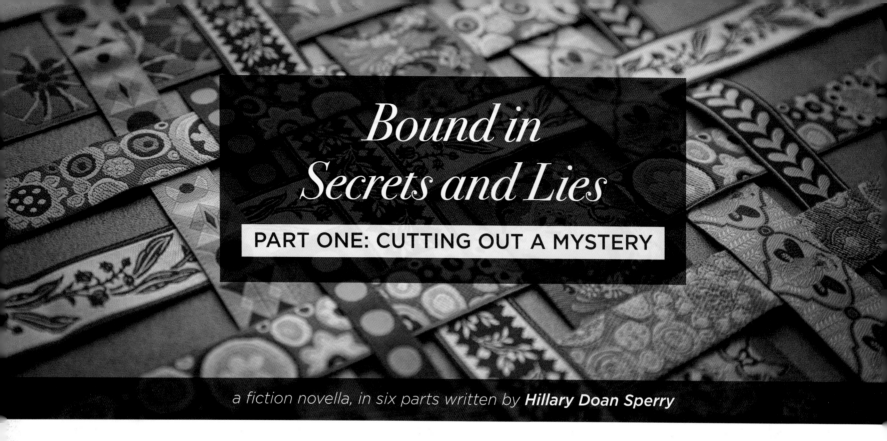

Bound in Secrets and Lies

PART ONE: CUTTING OUT A MYSTERY

a fiction novella, in six parts written by **Hillary Doan Sperry**

Quilts billowed along the weathered grey boards of the old barn. The Antique Barn & Auction House's outdoor shopping venue was spread across the property of Jenny Doan's good friend, Grace Day. The old barn was the perfect backdrop for the beautiful pieces she had on display. They were all unique and lovely, but Jenny was looking for a particular quilt, one that Grace had shown her, a handmade pre-war sampler.

Behind her, Bernie and Dottie dug through a basket of vintage patterns while her new assistant, Cherry Carmine, lifted the corner of a bright floral-patterned quilt. The bright aqua in the accent corners matched the bicycles riding across Cherry's blouse.

"I sure wish one of these ladies would share their binding secrets with me. Mine always come out wrong." Cherry's voice had just a touch of a southern accent, and, even frustrated, her words had a warm tone to them. She let out a deep breath. Her strawberry blond hair fluttered across her cheek, and she let the corner drop.

Jenny laughed, taking the young woman's elbow. "Don't be shocked, but I've had my share of wonky bindings too."

"Not the great Jenny Doan." Bernie teased, pushing her glasses back into place and dropping a vintage ruler in her basket. "I didn't think Jenny made mistakes. Did you?"

She turned to her sister Dottie who chuckled. "I'm pretty sure all her quilts are stitched in silver and sprinkled in gold."

Cherry laughed, and Jenny shook her head at her friends. "There's no secret to binding. Just lots of practice. I should know. I've bound a few quilts in my day."

"When you don't, send them to me." Bernie teased. She and her sister reached them at the same time the owner of the antique barn appeared.

"Grace!" Jenny welcomed her. "I've been looking for you!"

Grace smiled back at her. "I'm so glad you accepted my invitation to come today."

Despite the warm welcome, Grace seemed tense.

"As if I wouldn't have been here anyway." Jenny offered, hoping her friend would relax.

"Jenny told me that this event is not to be missed," Cherry said, still admiring the wall of color alongside the barn.

Jenny squeezed the dark-haired woman and both Bernie

and Dottie gave Grace hugs as well before excusing themselves to keep shopping.

Walking down the row of antiques, Jenny remembered what she'd been looking for. "What happened to that quilt you showed me the other day? It was amazing. I was hoping to get a better look at it."

Grace flinched. "Did I tell you about that? I'm sorry. It's ... uh ... unavailable now."

"Oh." Jenny pulled back. She'd thought that was why Grace had invited her. "Did someone buy it? I guess I shouldn't be surprised. It was in perfect condition." Jenny had to work to keep the frustration off her face but she was sad to have let such a treasure slip away.

"It's not that." Grace rubbed at her knuckles and lifted a pleading smile to Jenny. "I feel so ridiculous. It's actually one of the reasons I wanted you to come. I seem to have misplaced it. No ... Jed told me I was losing things, but I'm starting to think—" Grace paused lowering her voice. "I think someone's been stealing from me. I might even know who."

Jenny's brow pinched in confusion. "What do you mean? Have you talked to the person? What are you going to do about it?"

"You don't understand." Grace glanced around and beckoned Jenny closer, tucking them behind a quilt. "Remember the accident the other day? Jed ran off the road, almost hitting me."

Jenny only knew a little about the young man. He'd been in and out of trouble for years, almost as long as Jenny had known him. "I remember. Didn't someone end up in the hospital?"

Grace nodded. "The passenger, Charlie Reyes."

"I hope he's alright, but I'm so grateful it wasn't you." Jenny put a hand over her friend's tight fist.

"I was very lucky. Charlie is my neighbor." Grace closed her eyes, and Jenny reached out, wishing she could do something. "He's alright. Home even, but poor Jed ... I felt so badly. Jed's car was destroyed, and his parents have run off again. I didn't have another choice."

"What did you do?" Jenny knew Grace and she worried the woman might have done something drastic.

"I offered him a room." Her voice was a mix of inevitability and frustration.

"That's a very nice thing to do." Jenny said, wondering if that was the big conclusion.

"I thought so too, except then he asked for money. So I gave him a job. Now things are disappearing. I don't know how to stop him."

Grace put a hand to her jaw, her eyes not focused on anything.

"Are you sure it was him?" Cherry asked. Her voice seemed to surprise Grace as if she'd forgotten anyone else was there, but with a slow breath, she confided in them both.

"I heard him at the back door earlier this week. He was telling someone how to get into the barn. And by the next day, I had several items go missing. From yard toys to the vintage quilt you mentioned. They're just gone."

"What did the police say?" Jenny asked.

Grace's eyes grew wide. "I didn't tell them. I can't."

"Why not?" Cherry seemed genuinely confused, but Jenny turned a knowing eye on her.

"Jed is her nephew." Jenny pursed her lips and turned back to Grace. "Even so. It's not okay to just let him go if he's stealing."

"Well, I don't think it's technically him." Grace pulled back, looking like a scared kitten.

Cherry moved forward, taking her hand. "Then he's helping someone steal from you, and it's not okay."

Grace's spine stiffened, and she stepped back from Cherry's hand. "You don't know what you're talking about. He's not taking advantage of me. I'm not senile. He's a young man down on his luck."

"I'm sorry, Grace. I didn't mean any harm." Cherry's accented tone only seemed to irritate Grace.

"You don't have to turn him in if you're not ready, but talk to him. Let him know that he's hurting you," Jenny said. She could see the moment Grace broke. Her brows pulled together, and she stepped away.

"I ... I have to go." Grace's nerves bloomed hives in large red patches across her neck. "My neighbor is supposed to be here." Grace moved into the aisle. "I need to go show her ... a clock ... in the barn. I shouldn't have said anything."

Grace's hurried departure left Cherry and Jenny in a silent limbo, questions in both their eyes.

"I thought I could help," Cherry finally said out loud.

"Don't feel bad." Jenny took Cherry's elbow and they walked toward the barn. "I agreed with you. I was surprised she got so upset."

"I don't even know Jed. I was the one that shouldn't have said anything." Cherry followed Jenny inside the darkened room. The bright sunlight of the summer day was thankfully cooler inside, but the aisles were so packed with vintage finds that they had to walk single file along the rows.

Cherry had only been working for Jenny as an assistant for a little over a week, and while she didn't know much about her, it was obvious that she was compassionate toward everyone that crossed her path. She'd hold the door for anyone with bags, pay for people's meals when they came to be short. Honestly, Jenny was surprised at how many times she'd already seen her helping others.

"Don't be too upset. Jed's been through a lot, but he's been in and out of trouble for as long as I can remember." Jenny paused, spotting the young man near the window at the side of the barn. He was speaking angrily to someone, though Jenny couldn't see who. She pointed him out to Cherry. "It looks like his trouble is just growing up with him."

She moved to turn the corner, but Cherry stepped closer to the window. "Isn't that Grace's neighbor?"

Jenny turned to see an unfamiliar middle-aged woman had stepped closer, shaking a bundled cloth at him. Jenny squinted at the woman. "I thought she said her neighbor was a man. Charlie something or another ... Reyes? I think?"

"Reyes." Cherry nodded. "That sounds right. That's Mena Reyes. She must be his wife then. She bumped into me when I first arrived."

Jenny watched the interaction for a second more before she shook herself and whispered to Cherry, "Come on. We're staring."

Cherry laughed, and they turned away only to hear Jed's voice rise above the chatter of the other customers. "This is her last chance to cooperate. She listens to me, but if Mish doesn't get what he wants, this is going to be bigger than a torn blanket. We've got to put an end to things."

Jed's growl would have terrified anyone, and though Jenny knew he was young, he towered over the middle-aged neighbor woman.

She responded, "You can't do this. Jed, he can't ask you to do this—"

"Who's Mish?" Cherry whispered, but Jenny didn't get a chance to answer because Mena, apparently, had eagle hearing.

Her gaze snapped to their faces and Jed's gaze followed. Before he met their eyes, Jenny and Cherry were hurrying down the aisle.

"Oh, my goodness." Cherry gripped Jenny's arm. "My heart is beating so fast."

Mish, Jenny thought and shook her head. They were just talking,

she reasoned. She didn't need to know about who.

She tried to focus on the dimly lit aisle as she steered Cherry toward the door. "It's a good thing it's none of our business," Cherry teased, "or we might have to go back there and ask some questions."

Her words brought Jenny to an abrupt stop, pulling a squeak from Cherry.

"You're right." The idea resonated, and Jenny could almost see Grace's distraught face.

"No. I'm just spilling nonsense. What do you mean? I'm right."

"We should go talk to them." Jenny turned and started toward the door. "If that had anything to do with Grace, we should let her know, and if it doesn't, then Jed's getting himself into trouble and it will affect Grace eventually."

Jed and Mena were no longer at the window, but that didn't stop Jenny. She moved quickly around shoppers and products. Suddenly, a crash sounded behind them, and from within the building, a resonating voice called out to exit the building. People hurried past as the crowd pushed Jenny to the exit.

The bright sunlight outdoors was shocking after the dimness of the barn. A magnified voice sounded near Grace's home, "This exhibition is being shut down. Return to your cars and don't make any more purchases."

"What in the world?" Jenny stood on tiptoe watching a head of slick brown hair weave its way through the crowd behind the bullhorn. "Who would want to shut Grace down? Is this what Jed was talking about?"

Cherry shrugged and Jenny gripped Cherry's arm. "I'm going to go find Bernie and Dottie. I'll be back."

"That's fine. I'll wait here." Cherry didn't sound disappointed at all to be left behind as Jenny pushed her way into the dispersing crowd.

The bullhorn and its owner continued to blast about leaving, and Jenny wondered briefly why Grace hadn't appeared. The auction house had gone from shoppers browsing to a mass exodus. Grace's business was being shut down, and she was probably still helping customers.

Jenny scanned the crowd and moved to a flower bed that had a little platform from an old well cap. She climbed on top and looked again. Bernie and Dottie were waving at her from the parking area, but there was still no Grace. A blast of sound right behind Jenny almost caused her to stumble off the platform.

"Everyone must exit the premises!" Shouted the man with the

bullhorn. His perfectly pressed suit was a bit much for the manual labor of shutting down a business. He watched the dispersing crowd but had his bullhorn pointed to her.

"Excuse me." Jenny attempted to get his attention as the man stepped through Grace's blooming violas. "I'm a good friend of the owner. Can I ask who gave you permission to shut things down?"

"We received a complaint," he said. Then as if to clarify, added, "I'm from the city."

Jenny could feel the skepticism pinch her face, and she shook her head at him. "That's all it takes? A complaint?"

"Ma'am, my name is Robert Holdin. I'm over city ordinances. I take these matters very seriously. Too many people in the space, parking violations, land complaints. There are a lot of issues. But we've got things well in hand. So, if your name is not—" He pulled a paper from his pocket and read the name. "Grace Day." He put the page back and looked at her closely with a tight smirk. "And, Mrs. Doan, we both know it's not. I'd appreciate it if you would return to your car and—" he held the bullhorn up to his mouth, "Go home!"

The crowd gave a subtle wave of movement around him as people backed away from the noise and Jenny clenched her jaw. Sometimes being well-known was a bit of a hindrance. Mr. Holdin kept the bullhorn to his lips, repeating several variations of the sentiment he'd bellowed before. If she didn't get clear of the man, soon her ears would ring like an old sewing machine in her head. She took a deep breath and looked around the crowd. Where had Grace gone?

Behind Mr. Holdin, a thin spiral of smoke rose from the back corner of the barn.

"What's that?" She asked, pushing past the hyper-focused man.

"What's what?" His oh-so eloquent response barely registered after the shouting. Jenny pointed to what had grown into a plume of black and grey.

"Oh my." The man stared to where she pointed. "Is that smoke?"

Someone screamed, and Jenny started running toward the building.

"Fire!" the word spread through the crowd like its own accelerant while Jenny pushed into the barn.
"Is anyone still here?" Jenny called out. A faint sound came from inside.

"Get away from there!" Jed's snarl caught her by surprise. She turned to see him barreling across the yard in her direction.

Smoke filled the room, and Jenny coughed, moving into the aisles. "Help me!" She called back to him. "Someone's still in here!"

"You're wrong. I've already cleared the building. You've got to go." Jed gripped the door frame, unwilling to follow her in.

"I heard a noise." Jenny ducked low, the room was hazy with the grey perfume of burning antiques. Wood and dust tangled in the stench of the flames.

Jed looked over his shoulder, nodded, and turned back. "Fine," he shouted after her. "It's your choice." And he ran, leaving her behind.

Jenny's lungs seemed to contract around the thinning oxygen. He really left. Jenny was shocked, but a shallow moan called her attention back just before another crash. Jenny bent low. *It's just smoke*, she told herself. *It's just smoke, and someone else is trapped in here.*

She couldn't see the flames, but she knew they were there … she heard a cough and followed.

"Hello?" Crouching, she tried to move quickly through the packed aisles, praying she'd be able to tell the difference between a person and a bucket of old linens. A movement behind her pulled Jenny around. Squinting through the pain of smoke in her eyes. She pulled her shirt over her mouth and nose as a filter.

"Where are you?" She called followed with a volley of coughing and dropped to her knees.

A crash sounded, and flames became visible in the back of the building. In a panic, she moved ironing boards and shoved piles of stuff to the side. Someone was there and she couldn't leave them, but she didn't want to die sifting through old ladders and vintage tchotchkes.

She dropped lower, spilling a bucket of wooden spools across the floor and exposing a worn sneaker. Jenny crawled closer, scattering objects until finally, she saw the face of a woman. She didn't respond to Jenny's voice but coughed as another crash sounded, and Jenny dropped to shield her friend's body.

"Jenny?" Beneath the crackle of flames came the croaking voice.

She waved at the smoke and whispered back, "Grace."

Flames shot through the rafters above them. Jenny was running out of time.

To be continued …

Southern Comfort Food
Ohio Starlight Mini Quilt

Southern food is like quilts. It's comfort. It's family. It's love you can taste, handed down through generations of grandmothers.

We asked Southern quilters for their favorite food memories, and the responses flowed in like gallons of homemade sweet iced tea:

"My grandmother taught me to quilt and make dressing. Both were a process of watching. No written instructions or recipes, just observing her ninety years of experience. 'I just do it like this right here' she would say. Now that she's gone, I make the dressing and the quilts for the family. My cousin, however, has carried on her gardening and canning skills. I think we become the things we love most about the people we lose. Grandmother is now so many little pieces in all of us. When we share those gifts with each other, she's still here with us."
— *Gipsy Osborne*

"There's nothing more Southern than biscuits. I have sweet memories of my great-grandmother making homemade biscuits. Every surface in her kitchen would be covered with biscuits. I couldn't wait for them to come out of the oven; those biscuits were divine! We ate them with butter, jam, honey, or syrup. My favorite was honey. I didn't need dessert with those biscuits dripping with honey! Now it's my turn. I have the privilege of making those biscuits for my own family. Best of all, I have Mamaw's biscuit cutter!" — *Jennifer King*

"We used to sit on the porch to snap the fresh-picked green beans. Then we cooked them up with bacon, onions, and potatoes." — *Cathy Haerter*

"I remember shelling peas during hot summers in Northwest Florida while Grandma cooked chicken and dumplings for supper. We always got a pot of field peas cooked as well for all our hard work."
— *Carol Pool*

Recipe shared by a Missouri Star reader

Sandra Hurley's
SOUTHERN CHESS PIE

4 eggs
1 can evaporated milk
1½ cups sugar
1½ teaspoons vanilla
½ cup melted butter
(real butter!)

Pour into unbaked pie shell. Bake at 350°F until a toothpick inserted in center comes out clean.

(**Note:** *Gramma's original recipe had twice the sugar and a teaspoon of salt. I've adapted it for our tastes.*)

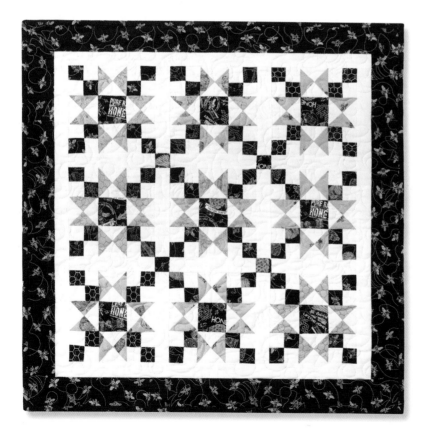

materials

PROJECT SIZE
26" x 26"

BLOCK SIZE
6½" unfinished, 6" finished

PROJECT TOP
1 package 5" print squares
¾ yard background fabric
  - includes sashing and inner border

OUTER BORDER
¼ yard

BINDING
¼ yard

BACKING
1 yard

OTHER
Clearly Perfect Slotted Trimmer A
  - optional

SAMPLE QUILT
Bee's Life by Tara Reed for Riley Blake

1 sort & cut

From the package of print squares, select 3 of the darkest squares for the star centers and cornerstones.

- Cut 2 squares in half vertically and horizontally to create (4) 2½" squares from each.

- Cut the remaining square in half once creating (2) 2½" x 5" rectangles.

  ○ Subcut 1 rectangle into (2) 2½" squares. Set 1 of these squares with the other 2½" squares for a **total of (9)** 2½" squares and set these aside for the star centers.

  ○ Trim the remaining 2½" square to 1½" square.

  ○ Trim the remaining 2½" x 5" rectangle to 1½" x 5" and subcut (3) 1½" squares. Add these to the previously cut 1½" square for a **total of (4)** 1½" squares and set these aside for the cornerstones.

From the remaining 5" print squares, select 9 medium squares and 9 dark squares for your blocks. Set the remaining squares aside for another project.

From the background fabric, cut (3) 5" strips across the width of the fabric. Subcut 5" squares from the strips. Each strip will yield up to 8 squares and a **total of (18)** 5" background squares are needed. Set the remaining background fabric aside for the sashing and inner border.

2 make hourglass units

Pair a 5" medium print square with a 5" background square, right sides facing. Sew around the perimeter using a ¼" seam allowance. Cut the sewn square from corner to corner twice on the diagonal to yield 4 half-square triangle units. Open each half-square triangle and press the seam allowances towards the darker fabric. **2A**

On the reverse side of 1 half-square triangle, mark a diagonal line corner to corner, perpendicular to the seam. **2B**

Lay the marked half-square triangle on top of the other half-square triangle, right sides facing with background triangles touching print triangles. Sew on both sides of the diagonal line with a ¼" seam allowance. Cut on the marked line. **2C**

1 Pair a 5" medium print square with a 5" background square, right sides facing. Sew around the perimeter. Cut the sewn square from corner to corner twice on the diagonal to yield 4 half-square triangle units. Open and press.

2 Lay the marked half-square triangle on top of the other half-square triangle, right sides facing with background triangles touching print triangles. Sew on both sides of the diagonal line. Cut on the marked line. Open and press. Trim to 2½".

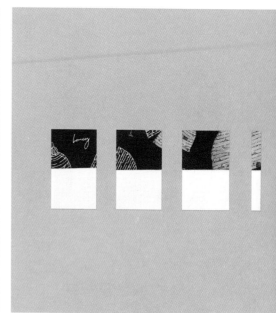

3 Take 1 set of strips and sew down 1 long side using a ¼" seam allowance. Repeat with the remaining sets of 1½" strips. Open and press each strip set towards the print. Cut each strip set into 1½ increments. You will need a total of 8 strip units.

4 Lay 1 strip unit on top of the other, right sides together, and print sides touching background sides. Sew down 1 side. Open to reveal a 4-patch. Repeat to create a set of 4 matching 4-patches. Square each unit to 2½" and keep the matching units together.

5 Select a 4-patch set, an hourglass set, and a 2½" center square. Arrange the units in a 9-patch formation, as shown. Sew the units together in 3 rows and press each row towards the hourglass units.

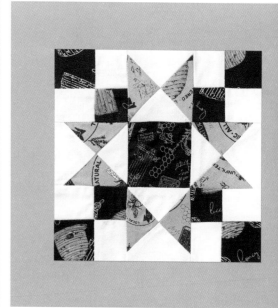

6 Nest the seams and sew the rows together to complete the block. Press. Make 9 blocks.

Note: When trimming, be careful to retain the corner points as you trim both sides of a corner.

If you are using the slotted trimmer, trim each unit to 2½", then open and press the seam allowance to 1 side. If you are not using the slotted trimmer, open each hourglass unit and press the seam allowances to 1 side. Measure each unit 1¼" from the center point and trim to 2½" square. Open each hourglass unit and press the seam allowances to 1 side.

Repeat with the remaining half-square triangle units to create a set of 4 matching hourglass units. Keep the matching units together. **2D**

Repeat with the 8 selected medium print squares and 8 background squares to make a **total of 9** sets of 4 hourglass units.

3 make 4-patches

Stack a 5" background square atop a 5" dark print square, right sides facing, on your cutting surface. Cut (3) 1½" strips across the width of the squares. Take 1 set of strips and sew down 1 long side using a ¼" seam allowance. Repeat with the remaining sets of 1½" strips. Open and press each strip set towards the print. **3A**

Cut each strip set into 1½" increments. You will need a **total of 8** strip units. **3B**

Lay 1 strip unit on top of the other, right sides together, and print sides touching background sides. Sew down 1 side. Open to reveal a 4-patch. Repeat with the remaining strip units to create a set of 4 matching 4-patches. Square each unit to 2½" if needed and keep the matching units together. **3C**

Repeat with the 8 selected dark print squares and 8 background squares to make a **total of (9)** 4-patch sets.

4 block construction

Select a 4-patch set, an hourglass set, and a 2½" center square. Arrange the units in a 9-patch formation, as shown. Sew the units together in 3 rows and press each row towards the hourglass units. Nest the seams and sew the rows together to complete the block. Press to 1 side. **Make 9** blocks. **4A 4B**

Block Size: 6½" unfinished, 6" finished

3A

3B

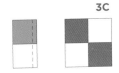

3C

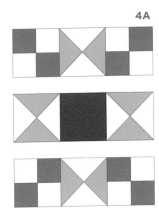

4A

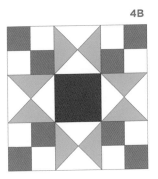

4B

5 sashing

From the background fabric, cut (5) 1½" strips across the width of the fabric. Set 3 strips aside for the inner border.*

*__Note__: If your background fabric is at least 43" usable width, you will only need (4) 1½" strips total and set 2 aside for sashing.

From the remaining 2 strips, cut (6) 1½" x 6½" rectangles from each for a __total of 12__ sashing rectangles.

Arrange 3 rectangles and 2 of the 1½" cornerstones set aside earlier, as shown. Sew the rectangles and cornerstones together in 1 long strip. Press the seams towards the background rectangles. __Make 2__ horizontal sashing strips. __5A__

Set the remaining 6 rectangles aside for vertical sashing rectangles.

6 arrange & sew

Refer to the diagram on page 55 to lay out the blocks in __3 rows__ with each row being made up of __3 blocks__. Place a vertical sashing rectangle in between the blocks. Sew the blocks and vertical sashing rectangles together to form the 3 rows. Press the seams of each row towards the sashing rectangles. Place a horizontal sashing strip in between each row. Sew the rows and horizontal sashing strips together. Press the seams to 1 side to complete the quilt top.

7 inner border

Sew the (3) 1½" background strips, set aside earlier, end-to-end to make 1 long strip.* Trim the inner border from this strip.

*__Note__: If you are using 43" background strips, cut (1) 20½" inner border and (1) 22½" inner border from each strip instead of sewing the strips end-to-end.

Refer to Borders (pg. 118) in the Construction Basics to measure, cut, and attach the borders. The strips are approximately 20½" for the sides and approximately 22½" for the top and bottom.

5A

8 outer border

Cut (3) 2½" strips across the width of the outer border fabric. Sew the strips together end-to-end to make 1 long strip. Trim the outer border from this strip.

Refer to Borders (pg. 118) in the Construction Basics to measure, cut, and attach the borders. The strips are approximately 22½" for the sides and approximately 26½" for the top and bottom.

9 quilt & bind

Layer the quilt with batting and backing then quilt. After the quilting is complete, square up the quilt and trim away all excess batting and backing. Add binding to complete the quilt. See Construction Basics (pg. 118) for binding instructions.

Talavera Tile Sew-Along
PART 1

Welcome to 2021's newest craze, the Talavera Tile Sew-Along! It's simply bursting with bright colors, pretty block designs, and plenty of fun. Inspired by beautiful Mexican pottery popularly known as "Talavera," this pattern is filled with sunny colors, reminiscent of warmer days and cool blue waters.

This quilt pattern came about during one of Missouri Star's last retreats in 2020. Sherrie Baker, one of our wonderful retreaters, designed a lovely quilt using several Missouri Star blocks and her quilt was the original influence for this new sew-along. Each of the blocks in this quilt are simple to make. They stand well on their own, if you would like more practice making them. All of the blocks for this quilt involve traditional piecing, but use easy methods with precuts. Get ready for a year of fabulous quilting fun with the Talavera Tile Sew-Along.

LEMON STAR (Block Only)

LEMON STAR BLOCK SIZE
31½" unfinished, 31" finished

BLOCK SUPPLIES - LEMON STAR
(6) 10" fabric A squares
(2) 10" fabric B squares
(2) 10" fabric E squares
(4) 2" fabric B strips
(4) 1½" fabric F strips
(4) 1½" fabric G strips

FULL QUILT

MATERIALS
QUILT SIZE
77" x 77"

QUILT TOP
1 package of 10" Talavera Tile squares* includes:
- 10 fabric A squares
- 10 fabric B squares
- 7 fabric C squares
- 14 fabric D squares
- 11 fabric E squares

¼ yard fabric B - includes Lemon Star border
¼ yard fabric C
1½ yards fabric F - includes sashing & Lemon Star border
3¼ yards fabric G - includes sashing, Lemon Star border, & binding

TOTAL FABRIC REQUIRED,
IF YOU ARE SELECTING YOUR OWN:
Fabric A - 1 yard
Fabric B - 1¼ yards
Fabric C - ¾ yard
Fabric D - 1¼ yards
Fabric E - 1 yard
Fabric F - 1½ yards
Fabric G - 3¼ yards

BINDING
¾ yard

BACKING
4¾ yards – vertical seam(s) or 2½ yards 108" wide

OTHER
1¼ yards medium weight fusible interfacing
Missouri Star Small Orange Peel Template for 5" Charm Packs

__Note__: 2 packages of 10" print squares can be substituted for the package of Talavera Tile squares. You will need a __total of (52)__ 10" squares. Other packages of squares may not have the same number of duplicate prints needed to match the quilt exactly.

1 cut & sort

From your package of 10" print squares, select 6 fabric A squares, 2 fabric B squares, and 2 fabric E squares.

Trim 4 of the selected 10" fabric A squares to 6½" and set these aside for the moment.

2 make half-square triangles

Lay a fabric B square atop a 10" fabric A square with right sides facing. Sew around the perimeter of the stacked squares ¼" from the edge. Cut the sewn squares from corner to corner twice on the diagonal. Open to reveal a **total of 4** fabric B/fabric A half-square triangles. Press the seam allowance toward the darker fabric. **2A**

Lay a fabric E square atop a fabric A square, right sides together. Repeat the instructions to **make 4** fabric E/fabric A half-square triangles. Press the seam allowances toward the darker fabric. **2B**

Layer a fabric E square atop a fabric B square, right sides facing. Repeat the instructions to **make 4** fabric E/fabric B half-square triangles. Press the seam allowances toward the darker fabric. **2C**

Trim each half-square triangle unit to 6½".

3 block construction

Pick up 1 of each style of half-square triangle and a 6½" fabric A square. Arrange the selected units in a 4-patch formation as shown. **3A**

Sew the units together to form rows. Press the seam of the upper row to the right and the seam of the lower row to the left. **3B**

Nest the seams and sew the rows together. Press the seam toward the bottom to form 1 quadrant. **Make 4** identical quadrants. **3C**

Arrange the 4 quadrants in a 4-patch formation as shown. Sew the quadrants together in pairs to form rows. Press the seam of the upper row to the right and the lower row to the left. **3D**

Nest the seams and sew the rows together. Press the center seam towards the top to complete the block. **3E**

Lemon Star Block Size:
24½" unfinished, 24" finished

2A

2B

2C

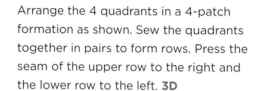
3A

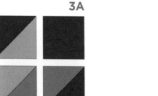
3B

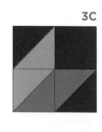
3C

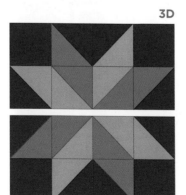
3D

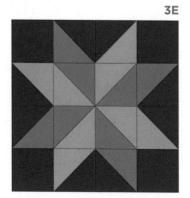
3E

4 inner border

From the fabric F yardage, cut (4) 1½" strips across the width of the fabric.

Measure the length of your Lemon Star block in 3 places. If needed, make any adjustments to your block so that it is 24½" long. Cut (2) 1½" x 24½" rectangles from the 1½" fabric F strips and attach them to either side of the Lemon Star block. Press towards the inner border.

In a similar manner, measure the width of your Lemon Star block and side borders. It should be 26½" wide. Cut (2) 1½" x 26½" rectangles from the 2 remaining fabric F strips and attach them to the top and bottom of the Lemon Star block. Press towards the inner border.

5 middle border

From the fabric G yardage, cut (4) 1½" strips across the width of the fabric.

Measure the length of your bordered Lemon Star block. It should be 26½" long. Cut (2) 1½" x 26½" rectangles from 2 of the fabric G strips. Sew these to either side of the bordered Lemon Star block. Press.

Again, measure the width of your Lemon Star block and borders. It should be 28½" wide. Cut (2) 1½" x 28½" rectangles from the 2 remaining fabric G strips and attach them to the top and bottom of the bordered Lemon Star block. Press.

6 outer border

From the fabric B yardage, cut (4) 2" strips across the width of the fabric.

Measure the length of your bordered Lemon Star block. It should be 28½" long. Cut (2) 2" x 28½" rectangles from 2 of the fabric B strips. Sew these to either side of the bordered Lemon Star block. Press.

In a similar manner, measure the width of your Lemon Star block and borders. It should be 31½" wide. Cut (2) 2" x 31½" rectangles from the 2 remaining fabric B strips and attach them to the top and bottom of the bordered Lemon Star block. Press.

Bordered Lemon Star Block Size:
31½" unfinished, 31" finished

Talavera Tiles Inspiration

Meet Sherrie Baker, the quilter behind the Talavera Tile sew-along! This marvelous woman came to a retreat, not knowing that her special quilt design would capture our hearts.

Tell us about yourself. Why did you begin quilting?
"I began sewing when I was nine on my aunt's Featherweight when I would visit her in the summer. I sewed my own clothes and doll clothes or little blankets for my dolls or dog. I started quilting about 12 years ago."

When did you make your first quilt?
"I decided to make my first quilt when my second granddaughter was going to be born. I was such a novice and didn't know anything about quilting. I chose fabrics from a big box store that were in different colorways of the same fabric. Since computer programming and Excel spreadsheets were very much a part of my work life, I drew out my design on an Excel spreadsheet. Instead of using different size pieces, I used thousands of 2½" squares. Oh what I have learned since that first quilt!"

What inspired you to create your incredible quilt?
"I absolutely LOVE Missouri Star! I live less than an hour away and visit as much as I can afford. From my very first retreat, I have made so many quilting friends. It truly is a family feeling when you shop, retreat, and go to Birthday Bash. When the line of Missouri Star souvenir fabrics came out, my friend and I saw them at Birthday Bash and we bought them without a plan. I soon decided to make a quilt from the Missouri Star fabrics to take to retreats. It seemed so fitting to be in Missouri Star fabrics. I also wanted it to feature common Missouri Star blocks from tutorials."

Do you have a name for it?
"Initially, it was going to be 'My Missouri Star Retreat Quilt' but after a booboo of sewing the last 2 rows turned the wrong way it is now called 'Finished is Better than Perfect.' It was supposed to be symmetrical with the smaller Missouri Stars in each corner. I didn't catch it until I had finished all the quilting on it."

What else would you like to tell us about your quilt?
"This was a great experience for me to design it, calculate everything out, and see it progress. The biggest payoff was Jenny's pure positive reaction to it when she first saw it last year. It was such a great feeling and when Natalie and Misty liked it also. I was on cloud nine!"

How does quilting help you express your creativity?
"Quilting can be anything you want it to be. It can be panels, piecing, paper piecing, thread art, and much more. Then adding in the different fabrics, colors, threads and the quilting designs, I can create anything. There are so many ways to quilt and there are no quilt police."

Is there anything else you'd like to add?
"I'd just like to say to any new quilters out there to not be afraid to jump in and start. Missouri Star has a lot of tutorials out there to learn from. Also, don't be afraid to go to a quilting retreat by yourself. You won't be alone past the front door!"

Quilting Across Cultures
Sashed Double Square Star Quilt

In Ancient Egypt, a pharaoh wore a quilted cloak. The beautiful lines of that garment are recorded in a 5,500-year-old ivory carving discovered in the Temple of Osiris. How I wish I could travel back in time to see the fabric!

More than 2,000 years ago, a quilted carpet was placed in a Mongolian cave tomb, an environment that kept it safe and preserved throughout the centuries.

And in the 1300s, a solid white trapunto wall hanging was created in Sicily. The intricate stitches tell the story of Tristan and Isolde, complete with battles, ships, and castles.

Quilting truly is a universal art with roots in countless cultures, both ancient and modern. I am so excited to share a few of my favorite examples:

Lakota (Sioux) quilters are known for their beautiful star quilts, or wičháȟpi owíŋža. Small diamonds are pieced together to create eight-point stars that represent the morning star.

This motif was traditionally used on painted buffalo robes, but by the late 1800s, the American bison had been hunted to near extinction and hides were scarce. Out of necessity, star quilts became a practical replacement.

In Sioux culture, a star quilt is often draped around the shoulders of the recipient to symbolize honor and protection on the journey through life. It is a precious gift that may be presented at births, graduations, and weddings.

In India, old saris are transformed into quilts called kantha. Several layers are hand sewn together using a running stitch called a kantha stitch. The result is a wavy, textured quilt that is said to provide safety, happiness, and prosperity.

Koreans have a centuries-old tradition of using colorful, embroidered patchwork quilts called pojagi to "cover, wrap, store, and carry objects ... They were used as tablecloths, to deliver a marriage proposal, to carry possessions on a journey, and to adorn and protect sacred writings. Women used pojagi filled with cotton batting and quilted to wrap fragile objects or cover food to keep it hot." (International Quilt Museum)

The Hmong people in Laos make an elaborate type of reverse appliqué called paj ntaub or "flower cloth." These maze-like patterns are often named for objects in nature such as elephant's foot, spider web, and water lily. Babies are wrapped in this intricate flower cloth, a disguise meant to confuse and thwart evil spirits.

As I learn about quilting traditions across the globe, I am reminded that we all have that inner spark compelling us to create. For warmth, for protection, for practical use, or for rituals, quilts make the world a more beautiful place.

materials

QUILT SIZE
53" x 53"

BLOCK SIZE
15½" unfinished, 15" finished

QUILT TOP
2 packages 5" print squares
2 yards background fabric

BINDING
½ yard

BACKING
3½ yards - vertical seam(s)

SAMPLE QUILT
William's Garden Batiks by Kathy Engle
for Island Batik

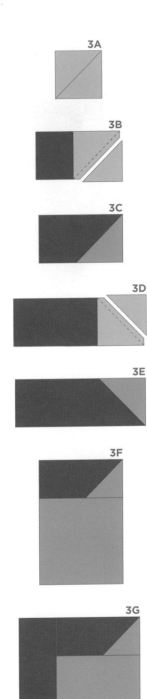

1 sort

Sort the 5" squares so there are 2 squares of the same color/print together. You will need 36 pairs of matching squares. Set the remaining squares aside for another project.

2 cut

From each pair of matching squares, cut (1) 5" square in half vertically and horizontally to yield 2½" squares. Each 5" square will yield (4) 2½" squares. Set (2) 2½" squares aside for the cornerstones. Keep the 2 remaining 2½" squares and the uncut 5" square of matching fabric together.

From the background fabric, cut (25) 2½" strips across the width of the fabric.

- Subcut 5 strips into 2½" x 5" rectangles. Each strip will yield up to 8 rectangles and a **total of (36)** 2½" x 5" rectangles are needed.

- Subcut 20 strips into 2½" x 7" rectangles. Each strip will yield up to 6 rectangles and a **total of (120)** 2½" x 7" rectangles are needed.

Note: Set 84 of the 2½" x 7" rectangles aside for the sashing.

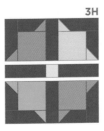

3 block construction

Select a set of 2 matching 2½" squares and a matching 5" square. Fold each 2½" square from corner to corner once on the diagonal. Press the crease in place to mark your sewing line. **3A**

Place a creased square on the right end of a 2½" x 5" background rectangle with right sides facing and oriented as shown. Sew on the creased line and then trim the excess fabric ¼" away from your sewing line. **3B**

Open and press the seam allowance towards the darker fabric. We'll refer to this as the short rectangle for clarity. **3C**

Place the other creased square on the right end of a 2½" x 7" background rectangle with right sides facing and oriented as shown. Sew on the creased line and then trim the excess fabric ¼" away from your sewing line. **3D**

Open and press the seam allowance towards the darker fabric. We'll refer to this as the long rectangle for clarity. **3E**

Sew the short rectangle to the top edge of the 5" print square, oriented as shown. Press the seam towards the square. **3F**

Sew the long rectangle to the left side of the unit, oriented as shown. Press the seam towards the square. Repeat to **make 36** corner units. **3G**

Select 4 corner units that feature different print fabrics, (1) 2½" cornerstone square, and (4) 2½" x 7" background rectangles.

1 Fold 2 matching 2½" print squares once on the diagonal. Place 1 creased square on the end of a 2½" x 5" background rectangle. Sew on the creased line and then trim away the excess fabric. Press towards the darker fabric.

2 Place the other marked square on the end of a 2½" x 7" background rectangle as shown. Sew on the creased line and then trim away the excess fabric. Press towards the darker fabric.

3 Sew the short rectangle to the top edge of a matching 5" print square, oriented as shown. Press towards the square.

4 Sew the long rectangle to the left edge of the unit, oriented as shown. Press towards the square. Make 4 units.

5 Arrange the 4 units, (4) 2½" x 7" background rectangles, and (1) 2½" cornerstone square in 3 rows of 3 as shown. Sew the units together to form rows. Press the seams towards the background rectangles.

6 Nest the seams and sew the rows together to form the block. Press. Make 9 blocks.

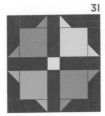

31

Lay the pieces out in **3 rows of 3** as shown. Sew the pieces together to form rows. Press the seams of each row towards the background rectangles. Nest the seams and sew the rows together. Press the seams to 1 side to complete the block. **Make 9** blocks. **3H 3I**

Block Size: 15½" unfinished, 15" finished

4 make vertical sashing strips

4A

Select a 2½" cornerstone square and (2) 2½" x 7" background rectangles from those you set aside earlier. Sew the rectangles to opposite sides of the square. Press each seam towards the background rectangle to make a vertical sashing strip. **Make 12** vertical sashing strips. **4A**

5 make horizontal sashing strips

Select (7) 2½" cornerstone squares and (6) 2½" x 7" background rectangles from those you set aside earlier. Be sure to select cornerstone squares of different print fabrics to add variety to your quilt. Alternate the squares and rectangles and sew them together to form a long horizontal sashing strip. Press the seams towards the background rectangles. **Make 4** horizontal sashing strips. **5A**

6 arrange & sew

Refer to the diagram on the bottom left to lay out the blocks in **3 rows** with each row being made up of **3 blocks**. Place a vertical sashing strip in between each block and on both ends. Sew the blocks and vertical sashing strips together to form the 3 rows. Press the seams of each row towards the sashing strips.

Place a horizontal sashing strip in between each row and on the top and bottom. Sew the rows and horizontal sashing strips together. Press the seams to 1 side to complete the quilt top.

7 quilt & bind

Layer the quilt with batting and backing then quilt. After the quilting is complete, square up the quilt and trim away all excess batting and backing. Add binding to complete the quilt. See Construction Basics (pg. 118) for binding instructions.

5A

Quilting is My Happy Place
Sew Inspired Quilt

A rain shower might spoil the day if you are hoping to plant a garden. Gloomy clouds can cast a shadow on picnics and soccer games and walks in the park. But when it comes to quilting, dreary weather is simply the best! I love to stitch the day away as the rain taps a happy rhythm on my sewing room window.

Now, I know that every sewing space is unique. Some of us quilt in a big, fancy studio. Others find room on one corner of the dining room table. But no matter what it looks like, your sewing space can be a haven of creativity and peace, especially when skies are gray,

I chatted with a lovely group of quilters to ask about their sewing spaces, and here's what they had to say:

"I call my sewing room my happy place. When I get cranky, my husband sends me there for a time-out. I always have three projects going at the same time. One on the cutting table, one on my piecing machine, and one on my Sweet Sixteen longarm machine. Things get chaotic at times, but I don't share the space with anyone, so I can leave my mess and come back to where I left off. When I find myself having to look for something, I take an hour or two to put things back in order just so I can create more chaos ... and quilts, of course!"
— *Georgia McCroy*

"My sewing room is my escape room. It is my happy place. All the worries of life are left at the door."
— *Pat DeBroeck*

"My sewing room is in the back of the house where it's very quiet. There are two big windows that let in lots of light. The hum of my sewing machine makes me happy. So does my big design wall where I keep some of my favorite projects' blocks up. My fabrics and patterns are organized. Sometimes I just sit on the floor and play with fabric and designs for hours! It's my HAPPY PLACE!"
— *Phyllis Studt*

"My roommate and I live in a small apartment in town, so my sewing room is the living room. While I sew, I get to listen to him watch tv or play video games. I found a fabric table that can fold up to be stored or used as a shelf. Fabric is stored in flat totes under a bed and current projects stay in a decorative tote by my sewing machine. My design wall is always up and covered with my latest blocks. It's like art that is ever-changing. I use small folding end tables to iron and cut. They get folded up when not in use. Best of all, I sit in a gaming chair with a built-in massage function, so I can sit for hours and be comfy, and any time I want, I turn my chair and start gaming." — *Joshua Poole*

"My sewing space is part of the laundry room. No one wants to get put to work, so it's all mine and peaceful! I'm one happy mamma!" — *Ros MacIsaac*

"My sewing space is a chaotic haven. I'm surrounded by piles of fabric and I love it!" — *Jocelyn Galloway*

"Due to lockdown and working from home, I don't have a sewing room at the moment. Instead, I have taken over the dining room table. You work with what you have. I'm grateful for the space I have to create. I try to keep it cleaned up and organized and leave room for breakfast."
— *Peggy Ramey-Renk*

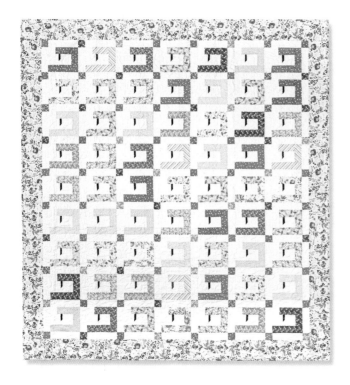

materials

QUILT SIZE
86½" x 94"

BLOCK SIZE
9" x 7½" unfinished,
8½" x 7" finished

QUILT TOP
1 roll 2½" print strips
¼ yard solid black fabric
1 roll 2½" background strips
  - includes sashing
1¼ yards background fabric

BORDER
1¾ yards

BINDING
¾ yard

BACKING
8½ yards - vertical seam(s)
  or 3 yards of 108" wide

SAMPLE QUILT
Cora by Tessie Fay
  for Windham Fabrics

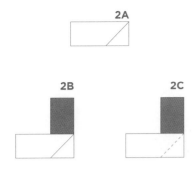

2A

2B   2C

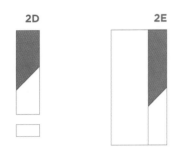

2D   2E

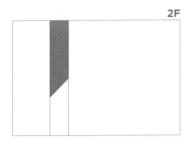

2F

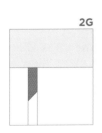

2G

1 cut

Select 32 print strips from your roll. Keep the print strips folded in half when cutting. From each of the 32 folded print strips, cut a 2½" x 5" rectangle, a 2½" x 5½" rectangle, and a 2½" x 9" rectangle. Sort the rectangles into sets of (1) 2½" x 5" rectangle, (1) 2½" x 5½" rectangle, and (1) 2½" x 9" rectangle. Each strip will yield 2 sets of rectangles and you will need a **total of 63** sets.

Select 5 print strips from your roll and cut each strip into (16) 2½" squares. You will need a **total of (80)** 2½" squares to complete the quilt.

Set the remaining strips aside for another project.

From the solid black fabric, cut (4) 1" strips across the width of the fabric. Subcut 1" x 2½" rectangles from the strips. Each strip will yield up to 16 rectangles and a **total of 63** are needed.

From the roll of 2½" background strips, select 11 strips and set the rest of the strips aside for the sashing.
- From 2 of the strips, cut 2½" x 1" rectangles. Each strip will yield 40 rectangles and a **total of 63** are needed.

- From 9 of the strips, cut 2½" x 5½" rectangles. Each strip will yield 7 rectangles and a **total of 63** are needed.

From the background fabric, cut (8) 3½" strips across the width of the fabric.
- From 1 of the strips, subcut (3) 3½" squares and (9) 3½" x 1½" rectangles.

- From 5 of the strips, subcut (12) 3½" squares. Add these to the 3½" squares you've already cut for a **total of 63**.

- From 2 of the strips, subcut (27) 3½" x 1½" rectangles from each strip. Combine these with the 3½" x 1½" rectangles cut previously for a **total of (63)** 3½" x 1½" rectangles.

- Set the remainder of the background fabric aside for the horizontal sashing.

2 block construction

On the reverse side of each 1" x 2½" background rectangle, mark a line as shown. The line begins in the top right corner of the rectangle and extends down and to the left at a 45° angle. **2A**

Lay a marked rectangle on top of a 1" x 2½" solid black rectangle with right sides facing and oriented as shown. **2B**

Sew on the marked line. **2C**

Note: You can remove the excess fabric by trimming ¼" from the sewn seam if you wish.

Open the unit and press the seam towards the darker fabric. Measure 3½" from the end with the solid black fabric and trim the unit to 3½" in length. **2D**

Sew a 1½" x 3½" background rectangle to the left edge of the unit. Press the seam towards the left edge of the unit. **2E**

Sew a 3½" background square to the right edge of the unit. Press the seam towards the right edge of the unit. **2F**

Select a set of matching print rectangles. Sew the 2½" x 5" print rectangle to the top of the unit. Press the seam towards the top of the unit. **2G**

Sew a 2½" x 5½" background rectangle to the left edge of the unit. Press towards the left edge of the unit. **2H**

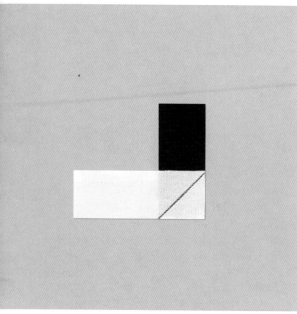

1 Mark a line on a 1" x 2½" background rectangle and place the marked rectangle atop a 1" x 2½" solid black rectangle as shown. Sew on the marked line. Open and press.

2 Measure 3½" from the black end of the unit and trim.

3 Sew a 1½" x 3½" background rectangle to the left edge of the unit and press. Sew a 3½" background square to the right edge of the unit and press.

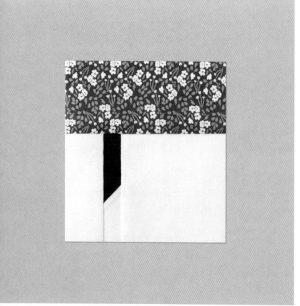

4 Sew a 2½" x 5" print rectangle to the top of the unit and press.

5 Sew a matching 2½" x 5½" print rectangle to the right edge of the unit and press. Sew a 2½" x 5½" background rectangle to the left side of the unit and press.

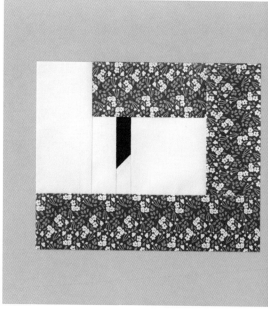

6 Select a matching 2½" x 9" print rectangle and sew it to the bottom edge of your unit. Press to complete the block. Make 63 blocks.

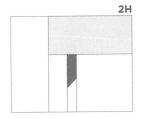

2H

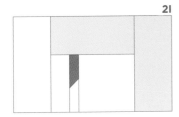

2I

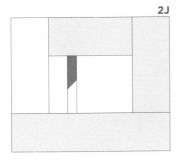

2J

Sew the 2½" x 5½" print rectangle from your set to the right edge of the unit. Press the seam towards the right edge of the unit. **2I**

Sew the 2½" x 9" print rectangle from your set to the bottom of the unit. Press the seam towards the bottom edge to complete the block. **Make 63** blocks. **2J**

Block Size: 9" x 7½" unfinished, 8½" x 7" finished

3 horizontal sashing

From the background fabric, cut (3) 2½" strips across the width of the fabric. Add these to the rest of your roll of 2½" background strips and cut:

- 1 of the strips into (2) 2½" x 9" rectangles and (2) 2½" x 7½" rectangles.

- 17 of these strips into (4) 2½" x 9" rectangles each. Add these to the other 2½" x 9" rectangles you've already cut for a **total of 70.**

- 14 of the strips into (5) 2½" x 7½" rectangles each. Add these to the other 2½" x 7½" rectangles you've already cut for a **total of 72.** Set these aside for the vertical sashing.

Pick up (8) 2½" print squares and (7) 2½" x 9" background rectangles. Be sure to select squares of different print fabrics to add variety to your quilt. Alternate the squares and rectangles and sew them together to form a long horizontal sashing strip. Press the seams towards the sashing rectangles. **Make 10** horizontal sashing strips. **3A**

4 arrange & sew

Refer to the diagram on the bottom left to lay out the blocks in **9 rows** with each row being made up of **7 blocks**. Place a 2½" x 7½" vertical sashing rectangle in between each block and on both ends. Sew the blocks and vertical sashing rectangles together to form the 9 rows. Press the seams of each row towards the sashing rectangles.
Place a horizontal sashing strip in between each row and on the top and bottom. Sew the rows and horizontal sashing strips together. Press the seams to 1 side to complete the center of the quilt top.

5 border

From the border fabric, cut (9) 6" strips across the width of the fabric. Sew the strips together end-to-end to make 1 long strip. Trim the borders from this strip.

Refer to Borders (pg. 118) in the Construction Basics to measure, cut, and attach the borders. The strips are approximately 83½" for the sides and approximately 87" for the top and bottom.

6 quilt & bind

Layer the quilt with batting and backing then quilt. After the quilting is complete, square up the quilt and trim away all excess batting and backing. Add binding to complete the quilt. See Construction Basics (pg. 118) for binding instructions.

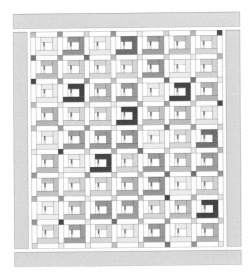

3A

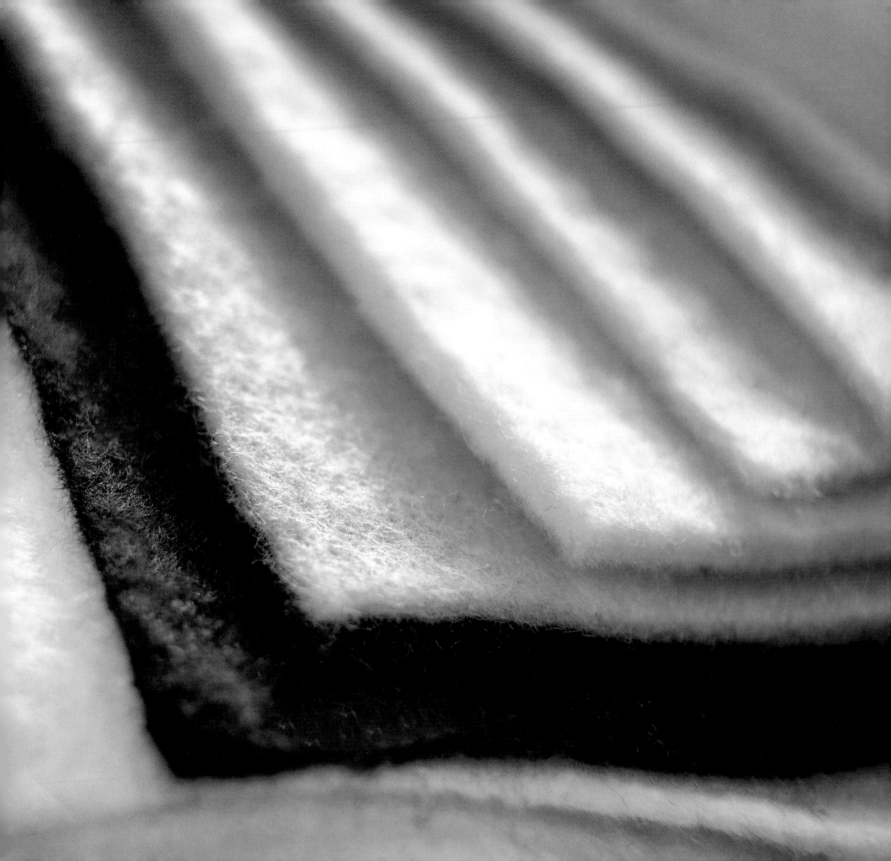

Foolproof Batting Tips for Better Quilts

Did you know that one of Jenny's daughters has her very own quilting tutorials now? The apple hasn't fallen far from the tree and now Natalie is here to teach us even more about finishing quilts—from creating your quilt sandwich to taking the final stitch. You can tune in to her tutorial series aptly titled, *"The Final Stitch with Natalie Earnheart"* on YouTube. Find yourself inspired as you learn new skills to help you put the perfect finishing touch on your beautiful projects.

One of the first subjects Natalie tackled in The Final Stitch was batting. Now, batting may seem simple enough, but sometimes we find ourselves stumped with the middle layer of our quilt sandwich. There are so many different types of batting and it may be challenging to know which kind to choose. Read on as we discuss common batting types so you can confidently select the right one for you! Then, check out Natalie's tutorial for even more in-depth information.

Common Batting Types

100% Cotton

This is one of the most popular kinds of batting for a reason. It's economical, it's easy to quilt, and it washes up well. Because it's an all-natural fiber, cotton batting has more weight per square inch than a synthetic fiber or a blended batting. With cotton batting, you can expect some shrinkage, and it is important to use high quality cotton batting without any stray cotton seeds, which can stain fabrics. If it's unbleached, cotton batting is naturally off-white with a few brown speckles that may show through lighter fabrics. In that case, go for bleached white batting. You can even use black cotton batting to match your project if it has a dark background. When you quilt cotton batting, make sure your lines or quilting pattern is closer together than 10" so that your batting doesn't bunch or shift. And when you're all finished, cotton batting will feel a bit stiff and needs to be washed and used quite a bit to soften it up.

80% Cotton 20% Polyester Batting

This type of batting is becoming increasingly popular and it's the kind of batting we use here at Missouri Star in our machine quilting department. It's truly the best of both worlds. Because it's a cotton blend with mostly natural fibers, it allows your quilt to breathe and washes up beautifully. The addition of 20% polyester fibers gives the batting additional strength to help it last the years and allows the quilt to drape beautifully. It also reduces overall shrinkage. It's easy to sew, easy to wash, and it's affordable. If you haven't tried it yet, we think you'll be pleasantly surprised!

"100% cotton batting is recommended for any projects that might be used in a microwave like heating pads or soup bowl cozies. Polyester is not suitable to be used with high heat as it can melt."

WOOL

100% POLYESTER

100% COTTON

80% COTTON/20% POLYESTER

BAMBOO

80% COTTON/20% POLYESTER

100% Polyester Batting

For those with allergies, this batting is a great option. Because it's synthetic, it doesn't irritate sensitive noses and it's very resilient even after frequent washing and heavy usage. It will last for years and is also resistant to mold and mildew. Polyester batting doesn't shrink as much as other kinds and it's available in many different lofts. The downside is that 100% polyester doesn't breathe like blended batting and because it doesn't shrink much, that reduces the pleasant crinkle effect we love in quilting. It can seem a bit too light and may not feel quite as cozy as a batting with natural fibers.

Wool Batting

If you're looking for a batting that's exceptionally warm and soft, wool is the answer! It has a fluffy loft, a lovely drape, it's easy to quilt, and it's a renewable fiber. Wool won't crease after months or even years of storage, but there are a few caveats with this type of batting. First off, it's spendy and natural wool batting tends to have a unique scent which may irritate those with allergies. It can also beard when you quilt it. That means, as your needle goes in, it may pull out a tuft of the batting out through the top of the quilt. Another challenge is shrinkage. Wool batting may shrink more than cotton, depending on how it has been processed, but you can find wool that behaves more like polyester and is easy to wash.

Bamboo Batting

You might say bamboo is the Cadillac of batting. It's incredibly soft, it has a wonderful drape, it dries quickly, and it resists mold and mildew. Bamboo batting hasn't been around for too long, just over a decade, but it's quickly gaining popularity like the cute new kid on the block. It's also a renewable resource, like wool or cotton, and it's very breathable and cool. It's lightweight, hypoallergenic, and more durable than cotton. It can shrink a bit, not any more than cotton, but the main drawback is it's pretty expensive. It's probably not the best choice for your first quilt project, but it could be just perfect for a family heirloom you want to last for years to come.

What Size Batting is Best for My Project?

Check out the free printable chart *msqc.co/battingguide* to see what size batting you need to finish up your next project. Missouri Star carries a wide range of batting sizes for table runners to king size quilts and even precut batting for our quilt as you go templates.

Hello Quilters!

I'm a big believer in journaling and keeping a quilt journal is a great way to preserve the stories behind your quilts, keep track of your WIPs, plan upcoming projects, and see your progress. For years, I had been keeping a notebook of my quilting projects and now I've designed a special quilting journal just for you! It's exactly what I want in a journal including a space to record the name of the quilt pattern, the size of the project, when you began it, when you finished it, who pieced the quilt, and who quilted the quilt. There is also a nice space to record any notes about the project, the story behind the quilt, and even add a photo, which I highly recommend. This handy quilt journal also has cute cover options with quotes like "She Believed She Could SEW She Did" and "Happiness is Handmade." When you take the time to record your quilting projects you're creating a keepsake for generations to come!

Jenny

"Putting on the Ritz" New Year's Eve mystery quilt, designed and taught by Sherrie Wohlgemuth, sponsored by the Cuts and Bolts fabric shop in Chillicothe, Missouri.

New Years Eve Mystery Quilt

For many years, way before Missouri Star Quilt Co. began, I have made a mystery quilt on New Year's Eve. I love the surprise of not knowing what I am going to get! About a month before the mystery sew-along begins, one of my favorite local quilt shops sends me the fabric requirements and cutting instructions. Then, on the morning of New Year's Eve, I get my first clue, and it is usually as simple as sewing two pieces of fabric together. From then on out, I get a clue every hour until the quilt is finished before midnight. It's a lot of fun for me and it's also a great way to learn new things and meet new people online. I love seeing all the different fabrics people use and how unique their quilts look. It helps me begin the new year with a surprise—the feeling that you don't know what you are going to get, but it is going to be great! That is how I feel about this year. We don't know what we are getting, but attitude is everything, and I am choosing to feel hope.

Design Meetings with Mom
Snowball Star Quilt

Quilting tends to run in families, through the generations, connecting us like the many threads that make up the quilt itself. Have you ever snuggled up in a family quilt and wondered who made it? How many babies have been rocked to sleep wrapped up in that quilt? How many family members have slept soundly beneath it? We may never know, but that quilt maker's legacy lives on. Teaching the next generation to sew and quilt is a wonderful way to continue the tradition and one of our younger readers, Kate Dorsey, shared this story about learning to quilt with her mother.

"Design meeting!' Mom calls from upstairs.

"I turn my eyes to the ceiling, wondering what she could possibly want to talk about this time. It could be about a quilt already in the works. Or something she came up with in the middle of the night. I won't know until she arrives.

"Mom comes down the stairs to the living room carrying bags of fabric. She also carries the pattern binder.

"The pattern binder. Now I know this meeting is serious.

"Mom drops everything on the couch and begins to talk about what has come to mind. She's my pattern tester and knows my patterns better than I do, creating version after version while I move onto different projects and ideas. The pattern binder contains every pattern she's tested, and some she has yet to try. It comes with us to the quilt shop, just in case we find a fabric for a quilt and need to know its requirements. When the binder comes to a design meeting, I know Mom has something very specific in mind.

"As Mom talks and shows me her idea, I stand and walk around the couch. I'm not leaving or ignoring her. I need the calculator to figure if what she wants to do is possible with the fabric we have on hand. Sometimes I can do this in my head. Other times I need the help of my calculator.

"While I calculate, Mom goes through fabric options. I agree with some. Shake my head at others. Offer suggestions. Back and forth we go as we get different ideas and show different fabrics together. Mom leaps ahead to possible borders while I say we should wait until the quilt center is done. It's our regular runaround as we work with two different processes to come to the same result. She plans far ahead while I work step-by-step.

"Decisions made, Mom packs everything up and takes it back upstairs. It could be days or weeks before we have another design meeting. Or it could be five minutes. The meeting may happen at home or in the car. It may happen truly anywhere an idea comes to mind.

"With our meeting over, I go back to what I was doing, and look forward to the next design meeting, whenever it comes around."

We have a feeling Kate won't have to wait long until the next design meeting with her mom! How do you like to share your love of quilting with the next generation? Share your stories at blockstories@missouriquiltco.com for a chance to be featured in BLOCK.

materials

QUILT SIZE
60" x 75"

BLOCK SIZE
15½" unfinished, 15" finished

QUILT TOP
1 roll 2½" print strips
1½ yards background fabric
 - includes inner border

OUTER BORDER
1¼ yards

BINDING
¾ yard

BACKING
4 yards - horizontal seam(s)

SAMPLE QUILT
Silver Jubilee by Maywood Studio

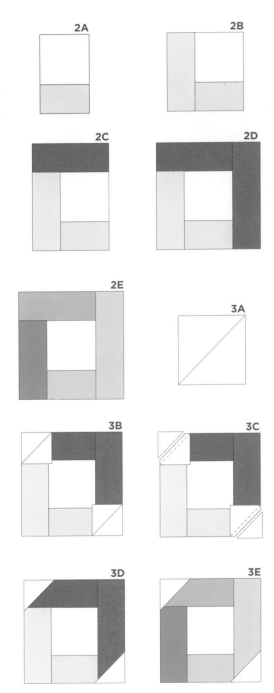

2A

2B

2C

2D

2E

3A

3B

3C

3D

3E

1 sort & cut

Sort your roll of 2½" strips into 4 groups. The groups we used for our quilt were made up of 9 dark print strips, 9 medium light print strips, 6 light print strips, and 6 medium dark print strips. You can sort your strips into like colors or values; it is entirely up to you and the strips you have in your roll. Leave all of the strips folded unless instructed otherwise. Set the unused strips aside for another project.

From your groups of dark and medium light print strips:

- Select 5 dark print strips and 5 medium light print strips and unfold them. Cut 2½" x 8" rectangles from the strips. Each strip will yield up to 5 rectangles and a **total of 24** of each color are needed.

- Pick up the 4 remaining strips from each group and refold them if necessary. Cut (3) 2½" x 6" rectangles to yield (6) 2½" x 6" rectangles from each folded strip. A **total of 24** rectangles of each color are needed.

From each of your 6 folded light print strips and 6 folded medium dark print strips:

- Cut (2) 2½" x 4" rectangles and (2) 2½" x 6" rectangles. Each folded strip will yield (4) 2½" x 4" rectangles and (4) 2½" x 6" rectangles and a **total of 24** of each size and each color are needed.

From the background fabric, cut:

- (5) 4" strips across the width of the fabric. Subcut 4" squares from the

strips. Each strip will yield up to 10 squares and a **total of 48** are needed.

- (12) 2½" strips across the width of the fabric. Set 6 of the strips aside for the inner border. Subcut 2½" squares from the 6 remaining strips. Each strip will yield 16 squares and a **total of 96** are needed.

2 make the units

Sew a 2½" x 4" light print rectangle to the bottom of a 4" background square. Press towards the light print rectangle. **2A**

Sew a 2½" x 6" light print rectangle to the left side of the unit. Press towards the light print rectangle. **2B**

Sew a 2½" x 6" dark print rectangle to the top of the unit. Press towards the rectangle. **2C**

Sew a 2½" x 8" dark print rectangle to the right side of the unit. Press towards the dark print rectangle. Use the dark and light rectangles to **make 24** dark/light units. **2D**

Repeat the previous steps to **make 24** medium light/medium dark units using the 2½" x 4" and 2½" x 6" medium dark print rectangles in place of the light print rectangles and the 2½" x 6" and 2½" x 8" medium light print rectangles in place of the dark print rectangles. **2E**

3 snowball units

Mark a diagonal line on the reverse side of each 2½" background square. **3A**

83

1 Sew a 2½" x 4" light print rectangle to the bottom of a 4" background square. Press. Sew a 2½" x 6" light print rectangle to the left side of the unit. Press.

2 Sew a 2½" x 6" dark print rectangle to the top of the unit. Press. Sew a 2½" x 8" dark print rectangle to the right side of the unit. Press.

3 Mark a diagonal line from corner to corner on the reverse side of (2) 2½" background squares. Place the squares on top of the unit and sew on the marked line. Trim the excess fabric and press open. Make 4.

4 Arrange the 4 units in 2 rows of 2, as shown. Pay close attention to the orientation of the units.

5 Sew the units together to form rows and press. Nest the seams and sew the rows together to form a block. Repeat to make 6 dark/light blocks.

6 Repeat the previous steps to make 6 medium light/medium dark blocks.

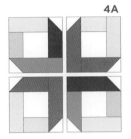

4A

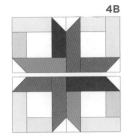

4B

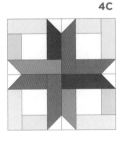

4C

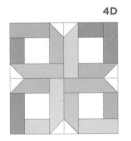

4D

Place a marked square on the dark corners of 1 unit, oriented as shown. **3B**

Sew on the marked lines and trim the excess fabric ¼″ away from each seam. **3C**

Press the seams towards the corners to finish snowballing the unit. Repeat to all remaining dark/light units. **3D**

Repeat the previous steps to snowball the medium light corners of each medium light/medium dark unit. **3E**

4 block construction

Select 4 dark/light units and arrange them in a 4-patch formation as shown. **4A**

Sew the units together in pairs to form rows. Press the seam of the top row to the right and the seam of the bottom row to the left. **4B**

Nest the seams and sew the rows together. Press the seam towards the bottom to complete the block. **Make 6 dark/light blocks. 4C**

Repeat the previous steps to **make 6** medium light/medium dark blocks. **4D**

Block Size: 15½″ unfinished, 15″ finished

5 arrange & sew

Use the diagram on the left to lay out the blocks in **4 rows of 3**. Notice that the blocks alternate between dark/light blocks and medium light/medium dark blocks. Press the seams of the odd-numbered rows to the left and the seams of the even-numbered rows to the

right. Sew the rows together and press to complete the quilt center.

6 inner border

Pick up the (6) 2½″ strips you set aside earlier. Sew the strips together end-to-end to make 1 long strip. Trim the inner borders from this strip.

Refer to Borders (pg. 118) in the Construction Basics to measure, cut, and attach the inner borders. The strips are approximately 60½″ for the sides and approximately 49½″ for the top and bottom.

7 outer border

From the outer border fabric, cut (6) 6″ strips across the width of the fabric. Sew the strips together end-to-end to make 1 long strip. Trim the outer borders from this strip.

Refer to Borders (pg. 118) in the Construction Basics to measure, cut, and attach the outer borders. The strips are approximately 64½″ for the sides and approximately 60½″ for the top and bottom.

8 quilt & bind

Layer the quilt with batting and backing then quilt. After the quilting is complete, square up the quilt and trim away all excess batting and backing. Add binding to complete the quilt. See Construction Basics (pg. 118) for binding instructions.

Quilts for Soldiers
Winter Star Quilt

Civil War Reproduction fabric has been a popular theme among quilters for a long time, and it's easy to see why! Deep rich colors, delicate florals, simple yet beautiful designs, what's not to love? But what truly makes Civil War fabric so special is a history that is as deep and rich as the colors it is printed in. The iconic designs and patterns of this particular fabric serve as a reminder of a time when quilts were as essential as medical supplies.

Sewing and quilting for a cause is no new concept—some consider it to be the very heart of the craft itself! In fact, selling quilts and sewn goods to help others and raise money was common well before the Civil War, primarily in the North. There, handmade goods were sold at great fairs and craft bazaars, usually as a way to raise funds for churches and schools. But when the war started and showed no signs of ending as quickly as many believed it would, the sewing efforts of Northern and Southern women alike went to the war.

Since many of the Union ladies had a fair amount of sewing knowledge and skills, their quilts were more elaborate. It's said that album, flag, and silk log cabin quilts were some of the most popular styles at the time! Beautiful quilts like these brought in a great deal of money that helped provide essential supplies for the Union soldiers. In the south, craft bazaars weren't nearly as common because many Southern women had servants who took care of all the sewing. But there were still some southern ladies who knew their way around a Singer! For example, the Confederacy needed gunboats, so some Southern ladies made what were called gunboat quilts. These were made from medallion style florals cut from printed fabric and sewn onto solid fabric, a method called "broderie perse." With the prices these intricate quilts went for, the south was able to afford a few ironclad gunboats. But as the war raged on for four devastating years, the quilts themselves became an essential need for both sides.

Soldiers needed blankets and cot bedding desperately, and all quilts donated had to be at least seven feet by four feet to fit the military cots used at the time. Being accustomed to sewing for a cause, the Union ladies got to work using all the available fabrics they had. Sometimes they would cut up two existing bed quilts and sew them into three cot quilts! It's estimated that by the end of the war, over 250,000 quilts had been made for Union soldiers. Southern women who weren't particularly skilled with needle and thread had a harder time aiding their soldiers with quilted comforts, plus the south couldn't get goods in through their ports and had no real manufacturing base of their own. But the ladies of the south knew their soldiers needed them, so they not only improved their sewing skills, they learned how to make homespun fabric and would even tear apart their own bedding and carpets to have fibers to spin!

Even with all the sewing these remarkable women did throughout the war, very few authentic quilts owned by Civil War soldiers can be found today. As you can imagine, these special quilts acquired a lot of wear and tear that probably rendered them unusable, and fallen soldiers were often buried with their quilts. It's a shame that it's so rare to come across such quilts, ones that were made with the utmost love by some devoted women. But that's why reproduction fabric is so well-loved—it reminds us of these women and of just how long quilts have been bringing comfort to those in need.

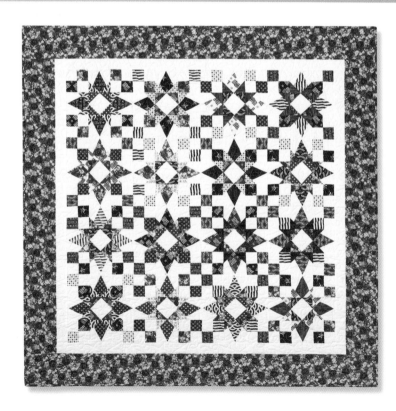

materials

QUILT SIZE
47½" x 54½"

BLOCK SIZE
6½" x 5½" unfinished, 6" x 5" finished

QUILT TOP
1 package 10" print squares
  - includes pieced border
1½ yards background
  - includes sashing

BINDING
½ yard

BACKING
3¼ yards - horizontal seam(s)

OTHER
Missouri Star Small Half-Hexagon Template
  for 5" Charm Packs & 2½" Jelly Rolls

SAMPLE QUILT
America the Beautiful by Deb Strain
  for Moda Fabrics

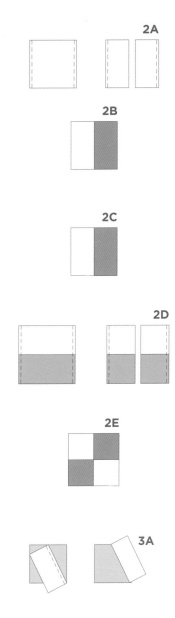

2A

2B

2C

2D

2E

3A

1 sort

Note: As you sort your squares, label each stack of squares for the appropriate section.

Choose (8) 10" print squares and (8) background squares for the 4-patches.

Select (24) 10" print squares and (16) 10" background squares for the snowballed star points.

Choose (4) 10" print squares and (4) 10" background squares for the square-in-a-square units.

Set the remaining 6 print squares and 14 background squares aside for another project.

2 make 4-patches

Take each of the print and background squares you set aside for the 4-patches and cut them in half vertically and horizontally to create 5" squares. You will need a **total of (32)** 5" print squares and a **total of (32)** 5" background squares.

Lay a 5" background square atop a 5" print square, right sides together. Sew down 2 opposite sides. Measure 2½" from the sides and cut the sewn squares in half parallel to the seams. **2A**

Open to reveal 2 strip units. Press the seam allowances toward the darker fabric. **2B**

Repeat to make 2 strip units using another 5" background square and a 5" print square of a different print. **2C**

Rotate the strip units 90° and place 2 strip units together, right sides facing, with the print strips touching the background strips. Sew down the 2 sides of the strip units, perpendicular to the seams. Measure 2½" from either side and cut the units in half parallel to the seams just made. **2D**

Open to reveal (2) 4-patches. Press the seam allowances of each 4-patch to 1 side. Repeat with the remaining strip units to make 1 set of 4 matching 4-patches. **2E**

Repeat with the remaining 5" print squares and 5" background squares to **make (16)** sets of 4 matching 4-patches. Set these aside for the moment.

3 make snowballed star points

Select 16 print squares from your stack of squares set aside for snowballed star points. Cut (2) 4½" strips across each square. Subcut each strip into (2) 4½" squares. Keep the matching squares together for a **total of 16** sets of (4) 4½" print squares.

Cut each of the remaining (8) 10" print squares into (4) 2½" strips across the width of the square. Subcut each strip

89

1 Lay a 5″ background square atop a 5″ print square, right sides together. Sew down 2 opposite sides. Cut the sewn squares in half parallel to the seams. Open and press. Repeat to make 2 strip units using another 5″ background square and a 5″ print square of a different print.

2 Place 2 strip units together, right sides facing, with the print strips touching the background strips. Sew down the 2 sides of the strip units, perpendicular to the seams. Cut the units in half parallel to the seams. Open and press. Repeat to make 4 matching 4-patches.

3 Lay a background rectangle atop the print square as shown. Sew ¼″ from the edge of the background rectangle. Press the background rectangle over the seam. Repeat to add another background rectangle to the opposite side. Trim the excess fabric even with the edges of the print square. Make 4 matching star points.

4 Lay a creased print square on a bottom corner of a star point unit as shown. Sew along the crease line, then trim the excess fabric ¼″ away from the seam. Press the snowballed corner over the seam. Repeat to snowball the opposite bottom corner. Make 4 matching snowballed star points.

5 Lay a print square on 2 opposite corners of a 4½″ background square as shown. Sew along the crease lines, then trim the excess fabric ¼″ away from the seam. Press. Repeat to snowball the 2 remaining corners using the 2 matching 2½″ squares. Square to 4½″ if needed.

6 Arrange the selected units in 3 rows of 3 as shown. Sew the units together in rows and press the seams in opposite directions. Nest the unit seams and sew the rows together to complete the block. Press. Make 8 of Block A. Make 8 of Block B.

3B

3C

3D

3E

3F

3G

4A

4B

4C

4D

into (4) 2½" squares. Each 10" square will yield (16) 2½" squares. Stack the squares into a **total of 16** sets of 8 matching squares.

From each of the (16) 10" background squares, cut (4) 2½" strips across the width of the square. Subcut each strip into (2) 5" x 2½" rectangles for a **total of 128** rectangles.

Mark the center of a 4½" print square by folding it in half and finger pressing a crease along the edge. Lay a background rectangle, right sides facing, atop the print square as shown—1 corner of the background rectangle at the center crease and the bottom corner on the same side of the rectangle, meeting the corner of the print square. Sew ¼" from the edge of the background rectangle. Press the background rectangle over the seam. **3A**

Note: If you prefer, after trimming each star point unit to 4½", you can fold the background sections over the seam and trim the excess fabric ¼" away from the seam. It doesn't add much bulk if you wish to leave it.

If needed, fold the print square in half again and recrease. Repeat the previous steps to add another background rectangle to the opposite side of the print square as shown. **3B**

Turn the unit over and trim the excess fabric even with the edges of the print square.

Note: If your background fabric doesn't quite go all the way to the bottom corners of the unit, it won't matter as this will be covered when the corners are snowballed. **Make 4** matching star points. **3C**

Fold each square of 1 set of (8) 2½" print squares corner to corner on the diagonal, wrong sides together, and finger press a crease. **3D**

Lay a creased print square, right sides facing, on a bottom corner of a star point unit as shown. Sew along the crease line, then trim the excess fabric ¼" away from the seam. **3E**

Press the snowballed corner over the seam. **3F**

Repeat to snowball the opposite bottom corner. **Make 4** matching snowballed star points. **3G**

Repeat to **make 16** sets of 4 matching snowballed star points.

4 make a square-in-a-square

From your squares set aside for the square-in-a-square units, cut each of the (4) 10" print squares into (4) 2½" strips across the width of the square. Subcut each strip into (4) 2½" squares. Each 10" square will yield (16) 2½" squares. Keep the squares separated into a **total of 16** sets of 4 matching squares.

From each of the 4 background squares, cut (2) 4½" strips across each square. Subcut each strip into (2) 4½" squares for a **total of (16)** 4½" print squares.

Select 1 set of 2½" print squares and fold each square corner to corner on the diagonal, wrong sides together, and finger press a crease. **4A**

Lay a print square on 2 opposite corners of a 4½" background square as shown, right sides together. Sew along the crease lines, then trim the excess fabric ¼" away from the seam. **4B**

Press each snowballed corner over the seam. **4C**

Repeat to snowball the 2 remaining corners using the 2 matching 2½" squares. Square to 4½" if needed. **4D**

Repeat to **make 16** square-in-a-square units.

5 block construction
Block A
Select 1 set of 4 matching 4-patches, 1 set of 4 matching snowballed star points, and 1 square-in-a-square unit.

Arrange the selected units in 3 rows of 3. Make note of the placement and orientation of each unit. Sew the units together in rows and press the seams in opposite directions. **Hint**: Because the snowballed corners are on a diagonal, the snowball seams will not match the seams of the 4-patch along the edges. When you lay 1 unit atop the other, right sides facing, you can lift the edge of the top unit to

check and see that your seams will meet at ¼". If needed, make any slight adjustments and pin in place before sewing. **5A**

Nest the unit seams and sew the rows together to complete the block. Press the seams toward the bottom. **Make 8** of Block A. **5B**

Block B
Again, select 1 set of 4 matching 4-patches, 1 set of 4 matching snowballed star points, and 1 square-in-a-square unit.

Arrange the selected units in 3 rows of 3. Make note of the placement and orientation of each unit. On this block the 4-patches will have prints next to the snowballed star points. Sew the units together in rows and press the seams in opposite directions. **5C**

Nest the unit seams and sew the rows together to complete the block. Press the seams toward the bottom. **Make 8** of Block B. **5D**

Block Size: 12½" unfinished, 12" finished

6 arrange & sew
Refer to the diagram on page 93 as necessary to lay out your units in **4 rows** of **4 blocks**. Rows 1 and 3 will begin with a Block A and alternate with Block B. Rows 2 and 4 will begin with a Block B and alternate with Block A. Sew the blocks together in rows. Press the seam allowances of rows 1 and 3 to the left and rows 2 and 4 to the right. Nest the seams and sew the rows together. Press to complete the center of the quilt.

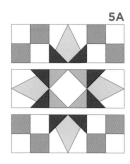
5A

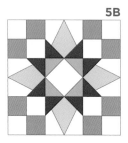
5B

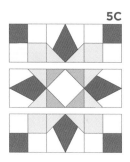
5C

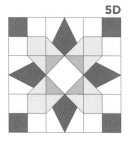
5D

7 inner border

Cut (5) 2½" strips across the width of the background fabric. Sew the strips together end-to-end to make 1 long strip. Trim the inner borders from this strip.

Refer to Borders (pg. 118) in the Construction Basics to measure, cut, and attach the inner borders. The strips are approximately 48½" for the sides and approximately 52½" for the top and bottom.

8 outer border

Cut (6) 6" strips across the width of the outer border fabric. Sew the strips together end-to-end to make 1 long strip. Trim the outer borders from this strip.

Refer to Borders (pg. 118) in the Construction Basics to measure, cut, and attach the outer borders. The strips are approximately 52½" for the sides and approximately 63½" for the top and bottom.

9 quilt & bind

Layer the quilt with batting and backing and quilt. After the quilting is complete, square up the quilt and trim away all excess batting and backing. Add binding to complete the quilt. See Construction Basics (pg. 118) for binding instructions.

Love Blooms Here
Grow Your Garden Pillows

"Where flowers bloom, so does hope."
— *Lady Bird Johnson*

There's a lot of magic in hope. Believing that good things will come is part of what keeps us getting out of bed each morning. It's what gives us the desire to create, believing with all our hearts that we are adding beauty to the world. I love gardening for the same reason, I plant bulbs in the fall with hope, believing that they will come up in the spring, and they always do.

Creating anything is an act of hope. When we make things from the heart, we have the power to reach beyond our current situation to the future, sharing love and beauty for years to come. This story is from a reader named Cheryl Glander who has a strong desire to help others, which fuels her hope. How do you find hope in quilting? Share your stories with us at blockstories@ missouriquiltco.com

"I guess that I've always been a doer. My mama taught me, 'Do unto others as you would have them do unto to you.' When I was a Girl Scout, I was always trying to earn another badge. Our group of girls worked hard to learn another skill that usually involved charity work. Do I remember what we did? No. All I know is that these experiences shaped the values that I still use today.

"The first charity project that I remember doing came out of the love of my firstborn child, Amy. When she was in kindergarten she came home one day saying,

'Mommy! Mommy! Can you help my school?' Well it seems that the dolly bed in the kindergarten needed a new quilt and pillow. Thirty seven years later, I wonder if it's still there, and how many children cuddled their babies in it. I hope it brought comfort to those little ones, too.

"Time went by, I joined a local smocking guild, and was eager to share my talents in whatever way I could. During that time I became the chairperson for the Wee Care division of our guild. I smocked tiny christening and bereavement gowns for premature babies in the local hospital. There were times when the baby had nothing to be buried in, and our gowns filled the need, and comforted those who mourn them. Many years later, a friend of mine had a preemie that received one of our gowns. Her mother told me how much it had meant to them to receive this gown made from love.

"Since then, I have done other charitable projects. I have been in groups that knit hats and scarves for those in need and baby hats for preemies. Our local quilting guild is always making charity quilts, walker bags, and even dog beds for the local humane society.

"In the long run, it is the joy that keeps me going. Not only the joy of giving, but the joy I see on the faces, or notes from the recipients that receive these goods. Even if I never meet the person who receives what I have made, I go to bed knowing that I have taken one more step to make the world a better place."

materials

PROJECT SIZE
Fits 16" pillow forms

PROJECT SUPPLIES
2 packages of 5" print squares
¾ yard of background fabric for
   Pillow A
¾ yard of background fabric for
   Pillow B
¾ yard of background fabric for
   Pillow C
1¼ yards of backing
2 yards of Heat n Bond Lite

TEMPLATES - OPTIONAL
Missouri Star Petal Template for
   5" Squares
Missouri Star Mini Periwinkle
   (Wacky Web) Template for
   2.5" Squares
Missouri Star Small Orange Peel
   Template for 5" Charm Packs

OPTIONAL PILLOW INSERTS
1½ yards of muslin for 3 inserts
   or ½ yard per single insert
Fiberfill

SAMPLE PROJECT
Sanctuary by 3 Sisters
   for Moda Fabrics

2A

1 sort & cut

Sort the packages of 5" print squares into groups by color. Your squares may have several different shades and other colors mixed in. Put them in the color pile that is the most prominent in each square.

From each of the background fabrics, cut a 16" strip across the width of the fabric. Subcut (1) 16" square and (2) 16" x 12" rectangles from each strip.

From the remainder of the Pillow A background, cut a 4¼" strip across the width of the fabric. Subcut a 4¼" square from the strip and set it aside for the Pillow A flower center circle. Trim the remainder of the strip to 1¼" and set this aside for the Pillow B flower center circles.

From the remainder of the Pillow C background, cut a 3¼" strip across the width of the fabric. Subcut (1) 3¼" square and set it aside for the Pillow C flower center.

From the backing fabric, cut (2) 19" strips across the width of the fabric. Subcut (2) 19" squares from 1 strip and (1) 19" square from the other strip for a **total of 3**.

2 make the pillow tops

These pillows are created using raw edge appliqué. The layout of each pillow top is different, but the basic construction method is the same. For each appliqué shape needed, trace the appropriate template onto the paper side of your fusible web. Roughly cut around the traced line and then follow the

manufacturer's instructions to adhere the fusible web to the reverse side of your fabric. Once the fusible web has adhered, carefully cut along the traced line. Peel off the paper backing and discard it.

Note: The templates we used to create each pillow in our quilt are on page 120. You can use the acrylic templates found on the supply list or you can create your own shape. The template shapes are meant to be a starting point. Feel free to modify them to your liking. The templates for the leaf and flower center shapes can be found on page 116.

For Pillow A, you will need:
• 12 petal shapes cut from 12 print squares of 1 color group.

• 3 leaf shapes cut from 3 print squares of 1 color group.

• (1) 3¾" flower center circle shape cut from the 4¼" Pillow A background square.

For Pillow B, you will need:
• 3 sets of 6 Mini Periwinkle shapes. Each set of 6 shapes can be cut from 2 matching print squares and the 3 sets should be from 1 color group. **2A**

• 6 leaf shapes cut from each of 6 print squares of 1 color group.

• (3) ¾" flower center circle shapes from the 1¼" Pillow A background strip.

2B

2C

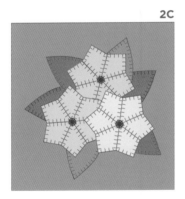

2D

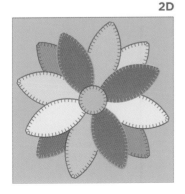

97

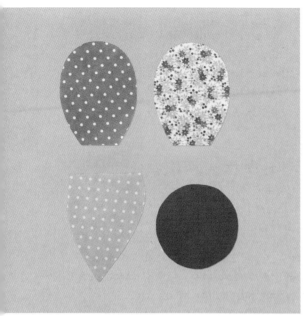

1 For Pillow A, you will need 12 petal shapes cut from 12 print squares of 1 color group, 3 leaf shapes cut from 3 print squares of 1 color group, and (1) 3¾" flower center circle shape cut from the 4¼" Pillow A background square.

2 Fust all of the appliqué shapes to the background square, and then stitch around the edges with a small zigzag or blanket stitch using a matching thread.

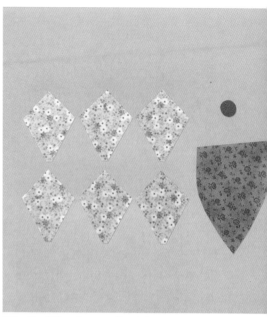

3 For Pillow B, you will need 3 sets of 6 Mini Periwinkle shapes cut from 2 matching print squares, 6 leaf shapes cut from each of 6 print squares of 1 color group, and (3) ¾" flower center circle shapes from the 1¼" Pillow A background strip.

4 Fuse all of the appliqué shapes to the background square, and then stitch around the edges of the appliqué shapes using a small zigzag or blanket stitch with a matching thread.

5 For Pillow C, you will need a Small Orange Peel shape from 12 print squares of 1 color group and a 2¾" flower center circle shape from the 3¼" Pillow C background square.

6 Fuse all of the appliqué shapes to the background square, and then stitch around the edges of the appliqué shapes using a small zigzag or blanket stitch with a matching thread.

4A   **5A**

 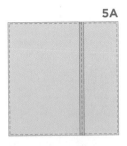

Pillow A

Pillow B

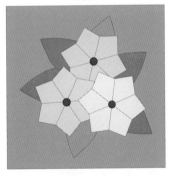

Pillow C

For Pillow C, you will need:
- A Small Orange Peel shape from 12 print squares of 1 color group.

- A 2¾" flower center circle shape from the 3¼" Pillow C background square.

The remaining print squares can be used for the bonus pillow that you can find in the digital version of this issue.

Once you have prepared each of the shapes needed for your block, refer to the diagrams on the left to lay them out on top of the appropriate background square for each pillow. Make any modifications or adjustments you like. When you're happy with the arrangement, follow the manufacturer's instructions to adhere the shapes to the background square.

After all of the appliqué shapes have been fused to the background square, stitch around the edges of the appliqué shapes with a small zigzag or blanket stitch with a matching thread. **2B 2C 2D**

3 quilt

Layer a pillow top with batting and backing then quilt. After the quilting is complete, square up the pillow top and trim away all excess batting and backing. Repeat for the other 2 pillow tops.

4 make pillow backs

Fold 1 long edge of a 16" x 12" rectangle over ½" with wrong sides touching. Press. Repeat a second time to enclose the raw edge of the fabric. Topstitch along the folded edge. Repeat on 1 long edge of each 16" x 12" rectangle. Keep the matching rectangles together to **make 3** sets of 2 pillow back flaps. **4A**

5 finish the pillows

Lay the A pillow top with the right side facing up. Lay the 2 Pillow A back flaps on top of the Pillow A top. **5A**

Note: The right sides of the pillow back flaps should be touching the right side of the pillow top and the pillow back flaps should overlap each other by about 5".

Pin or clip the pillow back flaps to the pillow top. Sew around the perimeter of the pillow using a ¼" seam allowance. Finish the edges with a serger or zigzag stitch to prevent fraying.

Clip the corners and turn the pillow right sides out. Insert a pillow form to finish your project. Repeat with the remaining pillow tops and pillow back flaps to **make 3** Grow Your Garden Pillows.

6 optional pillow insert

Don't have a pillow form handy? Simply cut (2) 17" squares of fabric and sew them together around the perimeter using a ½" seam allowance with right sides facing. Leave an opening about 4-6" wide for turning. Clip the corners and turn right side out. Stuff the pillow with fiberfill and whip stitch the opening closed.

BONUS
Rainbow Twine Pillow

materials

PROJECT SIZE
Fits a 16" pillow form

PROJECT SUPPLIES
Scraps of fabric in red,
    orange, yellow, green, blue,
    and violet colors*
1 yard of background fabric
½ yard mid-weight or
    heavyweight interfacing
(1) 17" square of batting

OTHER
Glue stick

***Hint**: Longer strips are easier
to twist, so scraps that are at
least 8" are best.*

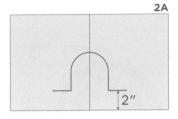

2A

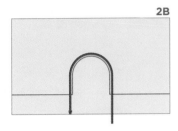

2B

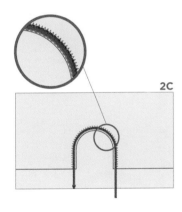

2C

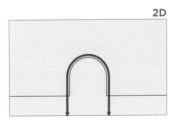

2D

1 make the twine

Cut or tear your fabric scraps into strips that are ¾" - 1" wide. Try to make your strips as long as possible because the longer they are, the fewer transitions between strips you'll have to make.

When you're ready, divide your strips into piles—red, orange, yellow, green, blue, and purple. It's okay if your fabric strips have other colors mixed in. Put them in the color pile that is the most prominent in the fabric strip.

Pick up 2 strips from the same pile and tie them together at 1 end. If the 2 strips are roughly the same length, cut 1 of them about 6" shorter. Place the knotted end in your non-dominant hand with the long strips resting in your lap. Use your dominant hand to pick up the strip that is farthest from you and twist it away from yourself 3 times. Once you've twisted it 3 times, lift it up and over the other strip. Now pick up the other strip and twist it away from you 3 times and then lift it up and over the strip closer to you. As you lift and twist the 2 strips together, you want to keep the twine loose enough that it is still flexible and tight enough that it will stay twisted.

Keep twisting and lifting the strips until the tail of your shorter strip measures about 3-4". When you reach that point, pick up another strip from your pile and fold or roll it a few times and then tuck the new strip into the end of the short strip. Carefully twist both strips as if

they were 1. Continue adding new strips as needed until your twine is to your desired length.

For this rainbow pillow project, you'll need:
- 1 length of red twine measuring about 3 yards
- 1 length of orange twine measuring about 2½ yards
- 1 length of yellow twine measuring about 2½ yards
- 1 length of green twine measuring about 2 yards
- 1 length of blue twine measuring about 2 yards
- 1 length of purple twine measuring about 1¾ yards

Bonus: Check out our tutorial video in the digital version of this issue

2 cut & prepare

From the background fabric:
- Cut (1) 17" strip across the width of the fabric. Subcut a total of (2) 17" squares from the strip.
- Cut (1) 11½" strip across the width of the fabric. Subcut a total of (2) 11½" x 17" rectangles from the strip.

From the interfacing, cut (1) 10" strip across the width of the fabric. Subcut (1) 10" x 17" rectangle from the strip.

Attach the interfacing to the reverse side of the 10" x 17" background rectangle. If you are using fusible interfacing, follow the manufacturer's instructions. If you are using sew-in interfacing, pin or clip the interfacing in place as needed and stitch around the edges to hold it in place.

Fold your interfaced rectangle in half to mark the center. Trace the template found on page 120 onto the right side of the fabric. The bottom of the template should measure approximately 2″ from the bottom edge of the fabric. You can extend the horizontal lines to the edges of the fabric if you'd like a longer guide. **2A**

Hint: A lightbox or window is handy for tracing the template.

Start with the knotted end of your purple twine and lay it along the curved edge you just traced. Leave about 2″ of tail past the straight line on the left side. **2B**

Set your sewing machine to a wide zigzag stitch and sew the twine to the background rectangle, as shown. Stitch along the outer edge of the twine. The zigzag stitch should fall in the center of the twine on 1 side and the background square on the other. Start and stop your stitching lines at the horizontal lines you marked on the background rectangle. Backstitch at both ends. **2C**

Cut the twine even with the background rectangle and then tie a knot at the end. **2D**

Repeat to add 3 lengths of each color to the outside of the arc. Stitch along both sides of the twine.* **2E**

*On the first purple twine you add to the rainbow, only stitch the outer arc. On the third red twine you add to the rainbow, only stitch the inside arc.

After you've added all of the twine to your rainbow, carefully cut around the perimeter of the rainbow and along the horizontal line you drew at the bottom of the rainbow. Gently peel up the twine along the edges to cut the background fabric underneath. Cut along the horizontal line you marked, so that the tails of the twine dangle freely. **2F**

3 make the pillow top

Pick up (1) 17″ square of background fabric and fold it in half to mark the center. Fold your rainbow in half to find the center. Place the rainbow on the background square approximately 4″ from the top of the square. **3A**

2E

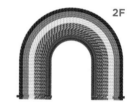

2F

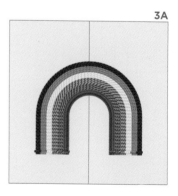

3A

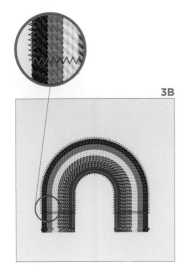

3B

4A

5A

When you are happy with the placement, place 1 hand on half of the rainbow to hold it firmly in place. Use your other hand to pull back the other half of the rainbow to reveal the backside. Apply just enough glue from your glue stick on the backside of the rainbow to hold it in place temporarily. Only apply glue to the background fabric that your twine is stitched to. Lay the glued side of the rainbow back on the background square and then repeat to add glue to the other half.

Use the same zigzag stitch you used before and stitch around the perimeter of the rainbow and cross over the tails even with where you stopped your stitch lines before. **3B**

After you've secured the rainbow to the pillow top, layer it with the batting and other 17" background square. Stitch the 3 layers together around the perimeter with a ½" seam allowance.

4 make the pillow back

Fold 1 long edge of an 11½" x 17" rectangle over ½" with wrong sides touching. Press. Repeat a second time to enclose the raw edge of the fabric. Topstitch along the folded edge. Repeat on 1 edge of the remaining rectangle to create the 2 pillow back flaps. **4A**

5 finish the pillow

Lay the pillow top with the right side facing up. Lay the 2 pillow back flaps on top of the pillow top. **5A**

Note: The right sides of the pillow back flaps should be touching the right side of the pillow top and the pillow back flaps should overlap each other by about 4".

Pin or clip the pillow back flaps to the pillow top. Sew around the perimeter of the pillow using a ½" seam allowance. Finish the edges with a serger or zigzag stitch to prevent fraying.

Clip the corners and turn the pillow right sides out. Insert a pillow form to finish your project.

6 optional pillow insert

Don't have a pillow form handy? Simply cut (2) 17" squares of fabric and sew them together around the perimeter using a ½" seam allowance with right sides facing. Leave an opening about 4-6" wide for turning. Clip the corners and turn right side out. Stuff the pillow with fiberfill and whipstitch the opening closed.

103

Disappearing Four-Patch Weave

QUILT SIZE
75" x 82½"

BLOCK SIZE
8" unfinished, 7½" finished

QUILT TOP
1 package 10" print squares
1 package 10" background squares

INNER BORDER
¾ yard

OUTER BORDER
1½ yards

BINDING
¾ yard

BACKING
5 yards – vertical seam(s)
    or 2½ yards of 108" wide

SAMPLE QUILT
Flea Market by Lori Holt for Riley Blake

QUILTING PATTERN
Loops and Swirls

PATTERN
P. 14

Double Square Star Four-Patch

QUILT SIZE
63" x 75"

BLOCK SIZE
12½" unfinished, 12" finished

QUILT TOP
2 packages 5" print squares
¾ yard accent fabric
1¾ yards background fabric

INNER BORDER
½ yard

OUTER BORDER
1¼ yards

BINDING
¾ yard

BACKING
4¾ yards – vertical seam(s)
  or 2½ yards of 108" wide

SAMPLE QUILT
Blue Stitch by Christopher Thompson
  for Riley Blake

QUILTING PATTERN
Birds

PATTERN
P. 20

Grow Your Garden Pillows

PROJECT SIZE
Fits 16″ pillow forms

PROJECT SUPPLIES
2 packages of 5″ print squares
¾ yard of background fabric for
  Pillow A
¾ yard of background fabric for
  Pillow B
¾ yard of background fabric for
  Pillow C
1¼ yards of backing
2 yards of Heat n Bond Lite

TEMPLATES - OPTIONAL
Missouri Star Petal Template for
  5″ Squares
Missouri Star Mini Periwinkle
  (Wacky Web) Template for
  2.5″ Squares
Missouri Star Small Orange Peel
  Template for 5″ Charm Packs

OPTIONAL PILLOW INSERTS
1½ yards of muslin for 3 inserts
  or ½ yard per single insert
Fiberfill

SAMPLE PROJECT
Sanctuary by 3 Sisters
  for Moda Fabrics

QUILTING PATTERN
Cross Hatch

PATTERN
P. 94

Hourglass Wreath

QUILT SIZE
77" x 93"

BLOCK SIZE
14½" unfinished, 14" finished

QUILT TOP
1 package of 10" print squares
  - includes cornerstones
1 package of 10" background squares

SASHING
1½ yards background fabric

BORDER
1½ yards

BINDING
¾ yard

BACKING
5¾ yards – vertical seam(s)
  or 3 yards of 108" wide

SAMPLE QUILT
Solstice by Sally Kelly for Windham Fabrics

QUILTING PATTERN
Drop of Paisley

PATTERN
P. 28

Ohio Star Celebration

QUILT SIZE
48½" x 48½"

BLOCK SIZE
11" unfinished, 10½" finished

QUILT TOP
2 packages 5" print squares*
  - includes cornerstones
1¼ yards background fabric
  - includes sashing

BORDER
¾ yard

BINDING
½ yard

BACKING
3¼ yards - vertical seam(s)

OTHER
Clearly Perfect Slotted Trimmer B
  - optional

SAMPLE QUILT
On the Go by Stacy Iest Hsu
  for Moda Fabrics

QUILTING PATTERN
Car Story

PATTERN
P. 36

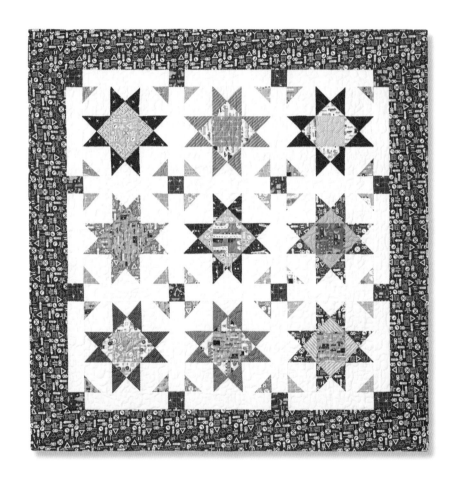

Ohio Starlight Mini

PROJECT SIZE
26" x 26"

BLOCK SIZE
6½" unfinished, 6" finished

PROJECT TOP
1 package 5" print squares
¾ yard background fabric
   - includes sashing and inner border

OUTER BORDER
¼ yard

BINDING
¼ yard

BACKING
1 yard

OTHER
Clearly Perfect Slotted Trimmer A
   - optional

SAMPLE QUILT
Bee's Life by Tara Reed for Riley Blake

QUILTING PATTERN
Buzzing Around

PATTERN
P. 48

Rainbow Twine Pillow

PROJECT SIZE
Fits a 16″ pillow form

PROJECT SUPPLIES
Scraps of fabric in red,
  orange, yellow, green, blue,
  and violet colors*
1 yard of background fabric
½ yard mid-weight or
  heavyweight interfacing
(1) 17″ square of batting

OTHER
Glue stick

PATTERN
P. 100

Sashed Double Square Star

QUILT SIZE
53" x 53"

BLOCK SIZE
15½" unfinished, 15" finished

QUILT TOP
2 packages 5" print squares
2 yards background fabric

BINDING
½ yard

BACKING
3½ yards - vertical seam(s)

SAMPLE QUILT
William's Garden Batiks by
   Kathy Engle for Island Batiks

QUILTING PATTERN
Jacobean

PATTERN
P. 62

Sew Inspired

QUILT SIZE
86½" x 94"

BLOCK SIZE
9" x 7½" unfinished,
8½" x 7" finished

QUILT TOP
1 roll 2½" print strips
¼ yard solid black fabric
1 roll 2½" background strips
 - includes sashing
1¼ yards background fabric

BORDER
1¾ yards

BINDING
¾ yard

BACKING
8½ yards - vertical seam(s)
 or 3 yards of 108" wide

SAMPLE QUILT
Cora by Tessie Fay for Windham Fabrics

QUILTING PATTERN
Spools of Thread

PATTERN
P. 68

Snowball Star

QUILT SIZE
60″ x 75″

BLOCK SIZE
15½″ unfinished, 15″ finished

QUILT TOP
1 roll 2½″ print strips
1½ yards background fabric
   - includes inner border

OUTER BORDER
1¼ yards

BINDING
¾ yard

BACKING
4 yards - horizontal seam(s)

SAMPLE QUILT
Silver Jubilee by Maywood Studio

QUILTING PATTERN
Snow Winds

PATTERN
P. 80

Talavera Tile

QUILT SIZE
77" x 77"

LEMON STAR BLOCK SIZE
24½" unfinished, 24" finished

BORDERED LEMON STAR BLOCK SIZE
31½" unfinished, 31" finished

QUILT TOP
1 package of 10" Talavera Tile
   squares* includes:
   • 10 fabric A squares
   • 10 fabric B squares
   • 7 fabric C squares
   • 14 fabric D squares
   • 11 fabric E squares
¼ yard fabric B - includes Lemon
   Star border
¼ yard fabric C
1½ yards fabric F - includes sashing
   and Lemon Star border
3¼ yards fabric G - includes sashing,
   Lemon Star border, and binding

BINDING
¾ yard

BACKING
4¾ yards - vertical seam(s)
   or 2½ yards 108" wide

OTHER
1¼ yards medium weight
   fusible interfacing
Missouri Star Small Orange Peel
   Template for 5" Charm Packs

SAMPLE QUILT
Circle Burst Wilmington Essentials
   by Wilmington Prints
Vintage Texture Wilmington Essentials
   by Wilmington Prints

QUILTING PATTERN
Free Swirls

PATTERN
P. 56

*__Note__: 2 packages of 10" print squares can
be substituted for the package of Talavera
Tile squares. You will need a total of (52) 10"
squares. Other packages of squares may not
have the same number of duplicate prints
needed to match the quilt exactly.

Winter Star

QUILT SIZE
47½" x 54½"

BLOCK SIZE
6½" x 5½" unfinished,
6" x 5" finished

QUILT TOP
1 package 10" print squares
  - includes pieced border
1½ yards background
  - includes sashing

BINDING
½ yard

BACKING
3¼ yards - horizontal seam(s)

OTHER
Missouri Star Small Half-Hexagon
  Template for 5" Charm Packs
  & 2½" Jelly Rolls

SAMPLE QUILT
America the Beautiful by
  Deb Strain for Moda Fabrics

QUILTING PATTERN
Stars and Loops

PATTERN
P. 86

Construction Basics

General Quilting

- All seams are ¼" inch unless directions specify differently.
- Cutting instructions are given at the point when cutting is required.
- Precuts are not prewashed, therefore do not prewash other fabrics in the project.
- All strips are cut width of fabric.
- Remove all selvages.

Press Seams

- Use a steam iron on the cotton setting.
- Press the seam just as it was sewn right sides together. This "sets" the seam.
- With dark fabric on top, lift the dark fabric and press back.
- The seam allowance is pressed toward the dark side. Some patterns may direct otherwise for certain situations.
- Follow pressing arrows in the diagrams when indicated.
- Press toward borders. Pieced borders may need otherwise.
- Press diagonal seams open on binding to reduce bulk.

Borders

- Always measure the quilt top 3x before cutting borders.
- Start measuring about 4" in from each side and through the center vertically.
- Take the average of those 3 measurements.
- Cut 2 border strips to that size. Piece strips together if needed.
- Attach 1 to either side of the quilt.

- Position the border fabric on top as you sew. The feed dogs can act like rufflers. Having the border on top will prevent waviness and keep the quilt straight.
- Repeat this process for the top and bottom borders, measuring the width 3 times.
- Include the newly attached side borders in your measurements.
- Press toward the borders.

Binding

find a video tutorial at: www.msqc.co/006

- Use 2½" strips for binding.
- Sew strips end-to-end into 1 long strip with diagonal seams, aka the plus sign method (next). Press the seams open.
- Fold in half lengthwise, wrong sides together, and press.
- The entire length should equal the outside dimension of the quilt plus 15" - 20."

Plus Sign Method

find a video tutorial at: www.msqc.co/001

- Lay 1 strip across the other as if to make a plus sign, right sides together.
- Sew from top inside to bottom outside corners crossing the intersections of fabric as you sew.
- Trim excess to ¼" seam allowance.
- Press seam open.

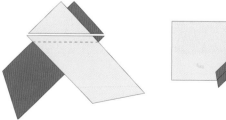
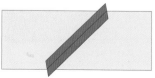

Attach Binding

- Match raw edges of folded binding to the quilt top edge.
- Leave a 10″ tail at the beginning.
- Use a ¼″ seam allowance.
- Start in the middle of a long straight side.

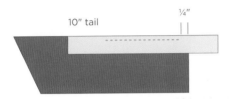

10″ tail   ¼″

Miter Corners

- Stop sewing ¼″ before the corner.
- Move the quilt out from under the presser foot.
- Clip the threads.
- Flip the binding up at a 90° angle to the edge just sewn.
- Fold the binding down along the next side to be sewn, aligning raw edges.
- The fold will lie along the edge just completed.
- Begin sewing on the fold.

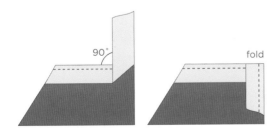

90°   fold

Close Binding

MSQC recommends The Binding Tool from TQM Products to finish binding perfectly every time.

- Stop sewing when you have 12″ left to reach the start.
- Where the binding tails come together, trim the excess leaving only 2½″ of overlap.
- It helps to pin or clip the quilt together at the 2 points where the binding starts and stops. This takes the pressure off of the binding tails while you work.
- Use the plus sign method to sew the 2 binding ends together, except this time when making the plus sign, match the edges. Using a pencil, mark your sewing line because you won't be able to see where the corners intersect. Sew across.

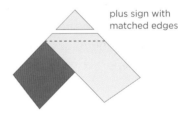

plus sign with matched edges

- Trim off the excess; press the seam open.
- Fold in half wrong sides together, and align all raw edges to the quilt top.
- Sew this last binding section to the quilt. Press.
- Turn the folded edge of the binding around to the back of the quilt and tack into place with an invisible stitch or machine stitch if you wish.

Pattern Templates

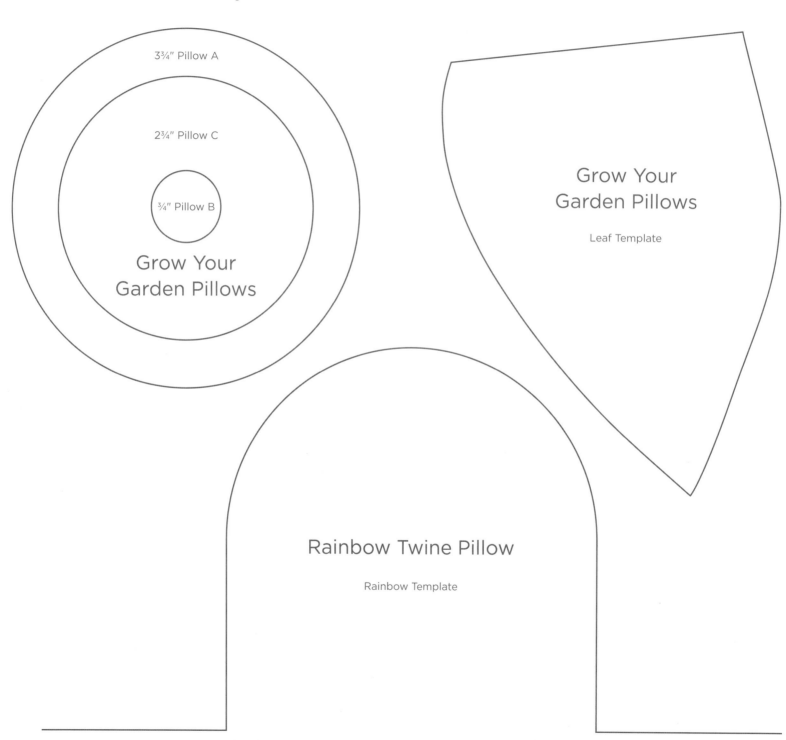

3¾" Pillow A

2¾" Pillow C

¾" Pillow B

Grow Your
Garden Pillows

Grow Your
Garden Pillows

Leaf Template

Rainbow Twine Pillow

Rainbow Template